ACADEMIC AND
LEGAL DEPOSIT LIBRARIES

THE EXAMINATION GUIDES SERIES

ACADEMIC & LEGAL DEPOSIT LIBRARIES, Donald Davinson

BIBLIOGRAPHY: HISTORICAL, ANALYTICAL & DESCRIPTIVE, Derek Williamson

DISSEMINATION OF INFORMATION, T D Wilson & J Stephenson

LIBRARY HISTORY, James Ollé

LIBRARY WORK WITH YOUNG PEOPLE, Stella Pinches

PRACTICAL CATALOGUING, W Dent

PUBLIC LIBRARY ADMINISTRATION, George Jefferson

SPECIAL LIBRARIES & INFORMATION BUREAUX, Roland Astall

THEORY OF CATALOGUING, Patrick Quigg

ACADEMIC AND LEGAL DEPOSIT LIBRARIES

AN EXAMINATION GUIDEBOOK

SECOND EDITION FULLY REVISED

BY DONALD DAVINSON BSC(ECON) DPA FLA
PRINCIPAL LECTURER, DEPARTMENT OF LIBRARIANSHIP
LEEDS POLYTECHNIC

ARCHON BOOKS & CLIVE BINGLEY

COPYRIGHT © D E DAVINSON 1965
ALL RIGHTS RESERVED
FIRST PUBLISHED 1965 BY CLIVE BINGLEY LTD
THIS EDITION COMPLETELY REVISED AND RESET 1969
THIS EDITION PUBLISHED IN THE UNITED STATES 1969
BY ARCHON BOOKS 995 SHERMAN AVENUE
HAMDEN CONNECTICUT 06514
PRINTED IN GREAT BRITAIN
208 00879 9

CONTENTS

CHAPTER ONE: HISTORY AND FUNCTIONS: *page 7*

CHAPTER TWO: GOVERNMENT, FINANCE AND ORGANIZATION: *page 36*

CHAPTER THREE: PLANNING, EQUIPMENT AND FITTING: *page 51*

CHAPTER FOUR: STAFF: *page 59*

CHAPTER FIVE: STOCK: *page 64*

CHAPTER SIX: SPECIAL DEPARTMENTS AND COLLECTIONS: *page 72*

CHAPTER SEVEN: RELATIONSHIP TO TEACHING AND RESEARCH: *page 81*

CHAPTER EIGHT: CO-OPERATION: *page 89*

INDEX: *page 98*

CHAPTER ONE
HISTORY AND FUNCTIONS

WHAT are the fuctions of a national library? A study of the declared aims of national libraries throughout the world will reveal no unanimity of purpose, but, rather, an interesting spectrum of purposes. In Holland the national library is concerned to build a research collection reflecting the best of the world's scholarship for the benefit of Dutch scholars. Apparently it is agreed in that country that other libraries are so effective in the collection and preservation of the records of Dutch culture, that the national library can be relieved of such responsibilities the better to concentrate upon non-Dutch collections. Switzerland, on the other hand, argues in the reverse direction, and maintains its collections solely as a repository of Swiss culture, leaving to other Swiss libraries the task of providing the materials necessary for research and teaching in other fields of knowledge. A similar motive activates the Hungarian National Library in its policy of selection of materials.

Most national libraries tend to undertake the twin functions of preserving the records of national culture and of providing an international research collection of high quality, with varying degrees of emphasis one way or the other. Thus the National Library of Scotland maintains that, while it has as its primary purpose the collection and preservation of the records of Scottish culture, it also has an important subsidiary purpose in the collection of an internationally based research collection for the benefit of all Scottish scholars and researchers. The National Library of Wales has a similar outlook, but goes all the way to provide for the national cultural interests by the production of *Bibliotheca Celtica*—an outstanding example of the central role of a national library in promoting the bibliographical control of a national literature.

The National Diet Library of Japan displays yet another concept of national library provision, by its co-ordination of the library services to all government departments as branch libraries of the central collection, with a unified staff structure, as described in 'The services of the National Diet Library' *National Diet Library news* (17) April 1963 1-4.

The study of the structures, roles and functions of the national libraries of the world reveals, then, a richly varied pattern. Sometimes the functions are devised to fulfil national needs, as in the case of Switzerland, where the formula can be seen as the natural expression of a desire to weld together the diverse elements of the heritages of the multi-lingual, multi-racial population. At other times, and more typically, the national library is the major research collection in a country, with an international coverage of the literature of general scholarship and research. Very frequently the national library takes the lead within a country in the provision of extra-national co-operative links, and assumes the mantle of leader of the nation's libraries through its bibliographical activities and research, and through development of advanced techniques of librarianship.

The major national libraries, such as the Library of Congress, the Bibliothèque Nationale, the British Museum and, from a purely British point of view, the National Libraries of Scotland and Wales, are all fairly well documented in the professional literature. However, it is, in fact, in other places than these that some of the most interesting activities in the development of a system of libraries based on the national library are taking place, and some of these ideas are detailed below.

A most important article considering the role of the national library is that by K W Humphreys in *Libri* 14(4) 1964 356-368. In this article the functions of national libraries are arranged in three broad groups, the fundamental functions, the desirable functions and the functions of a national library service which are not necessary functions of a national library.

1 *a*) The outstanding and central collection of the nation's literature.

b) Dépôt legal.

c) Coverage of foreign literature.

d) Publication of the national bibliography.

e) National bibliographic information centre.

f) Publication of catalogues.

2 *a*) Inter-library lending.

b) Index to location of manuscripts.

c) Research on library techniques.
3 *a*) International exchange service.
b) Distribution of duplicates.
c) Books for the blind.
d) Professional training.
e) Assistance to other libraries in library techniques.
f) Library planning.

A more succinct summary of the functions of a national library are those given in UNESCO *Bulletin for libraries* 18(4) July-August 1964 151:

1 To provide leadership among the nation's libraries.
2 To serve as a permanent depository for all publications produced in the country.
3 To acquire other types of material.
4 To provide bibliographical services.
5 To serve as a co-ordinating centre for co-operative activities.
6 To provide services to government.

The role of the national library received a thorough examination at the UNESCO symposium on national libraries in Europe held in Vienna in September 1958. The papers read at the symposium were later reprinted in book form as *National libraries: their problems and prospects* (UNESCO, 1960). Summaries of the papers and the principal conclusions reached also appeared in *Libri* 9(4) 1959 273-307, and in UNESCO *Bulletin for libraries* 13(1) January 1959 14.

In an article entitled 'The national library as a research institution' *South African libraries* 33(2) October 1965 41-45, A M Lewin Robinson provides a valuable definition of a national library. In summary he says: 'the principal difference between a national library performing its function as a research institution, and any other research library, is that the former is supported primarily by government funds with the intention that it should be for the benefit of the nation at large and not the privileged members of a district, a society or a university, even if the latter may be prepared to admit outsiders to make use of their facilities. Nor will it differ fundamentally in this respect from such magnificent private foundations as the Newbery Library in Chicago, though such a library can be more discriminating about its subject coverage. It will be expected of a national library that it will cover all subjects, even if not at the specialist level, and in theory this should be so; it is only the shortage of funds or the proximity of adequate special libraries that is likely to produce a less omnivorous approach, leading to a greater attention to subjects not satisfactorily covered elsewhere. In other words the national library, if it can not have everything, should at least be the source for material not found in other libraries '.

The *Parry report* pp 81-88 deals extensively with the functions of the national library under headings broadly similar to those in the article by K W Humphreys mentioned above. Perhaps the most exciting and clearly argued view of the functions of the national library is, however, G T Alley's ' The national library in the social process ' *New Zealand libraries* 30(5) October 1967 141-156. Mr Alley is the National Librarian of New Zealand, and he makes a clear case for the national library being what he terms ' the focus of leadership ' of the nations libraries.

COMPARISON OF NATIONAL LIBRARY FUNCTIONS

The study of the functions and purposes of the various individual national libraries of the world can conveniently be begun through *National libraries of the world* (Library Association, 1957), which is the second edition of a work by Arundel Esdaile, in this case edited by F J Hill. Although obviously dated, the work is valuable historically and is still the only substantial source of information in English about the services and nature of the national libraries of some of the lesser known countries.

Many writers on national libraries see their ideal circumstances as being those in which they are the centre of a network of libraries within their respective countries, guiding, inspiring and experimenting, being the sheet-anchor of a national and international system of co-operation, producing basic bibliography, and providing scope for the training of the future leaders of the profession of librarianship. Knud Larsen, in his *National bibliographical services* (UNESCO, 1955) drew up a blueprint for such a close knit system, in a work which has had considerable influence upon the evolution of national libraries and national library services in the developing countries.

In Britain the national libraries are, generally speaking, aside from the national system of libraries; they exist virtually as self-contained entities, thus depriving the system of some of the leadership so manifestly needed. The problem, recognized by the

Library Association in their *Access to information: a national bibliographic service* (Library Association, 1965), is not that all the essential functions of a national library service do not exist in Britain, but that they are, as yet, unco-ordinated.

The Library of Congress provides many of the services required by a fully structured national library system, but these are rendered, as it were, incidentally to their main purpose, and the library is not, by strict definition, a national library at all. The existence of so many other vast and rich research libraries throughout the United States results in a less pressing need for the husbandry of scarce resources by the articulation of careful policies of co-ordination and control. Despite this, however, it is a fact that the United States does have some very interesting and useful 'husbandry' schemes, as will be seen in chapter eight.

The Lenin Library in Moscow is, possibly, of the great national libraries of the world, the most fully integrated into the national system of libraries. The Lenin Library provides a bibliographic clearing house, lends from its own stock, has drawn up a widely used classification scheme and houses a large library school. The Bibliothèque Nationale in Paris occupies a midway position between the highly integrated situation of the Lenin Library and the relative exclusiveness of the British Museum Library, being a centre for international exchange and inter-library co-operation, and a clearing house for bibliographical information.

It is to some of the smaller European national libraries and to some of the developing national libraries in the 'emerging' parts of the world—Africa and Asia—that we must turn to see the pattern of integration into the national system of libraries being fully worked out. The Albert I Royal and National Library of Belgium, in its recently completed new buildings, is the centre for the collection and dissemination of scientific literature for the country, as well as being the national bibliographic centre. A similar situation of a combination of the Royal and National Library is to be seen in the Scandinavian countries where some such libraries also act as university libraries.

A summary of the history and present structure of some of the world's major national libraries follows.

THE BRITISH MUSEUM
The various collectors and benefactors whose works ultimately

found a resting place in the British Museum on its inception in 1753 are dealt with by Raymond Irwin in his article 'The approach to a national library in England' *Library Association record* 64(3) March 1962 81-93. The study of the growth of the British Museum collections must begin, where Irwin begins, in a study of the effects of the sixteenth century dissolution of the monasteries, which caused the dispersal of so much material that was later to be painstakingly re-collected into several notable libraries, such as those of the Harleys and of Cotton. These collections and that of Sir Hans Sloane were the most important of the basic collections. Other fine collections from private hands went into the museum's library at its beginning and in the years following, and a study of these, as of the whole history of the library, should begin with Arundel Esdaile's *The British Museum Library* (Allen and Unwin, 1946).

Most libraries of note can trace back their greatness to the inspiration of a single great figure. Bodley's re-foundation at Oxford comes easily to mind. The British Museum waited for nearly a century after foundation for its touchstone, in the person of Antonio Panizzi (1797-1879), called by his most recent biographer, G Miller, *Prince of librarians* (Andre Deutsch, 1968). An Italian who was forced to flee his country to exile in 1822, due to the injudicious expression of political views, Panizzi eked out a precarious existence as a teacher of Italian in Liverpool before securing an appointment, first part time but soon full time, at the British Museum in 1831. The poor state of the collections in the British Museum at the time, following years of largely inexpert handling, would have been a challenge to any person of even moderate energy. To Panizzi, endowed as he was with reforming zeal, it represented an irresistible spur, and he rose rapidly in the hierarchy, becoming keeper of Printed Books in 1837 and, finally, Director and Principal Librarian from 1856-1866. His lasting influence is to be seen in his formulation of the famous ' 91 rules ' —the British Museum cataloguing code—in his inception of the programme which led to the great printed catalogue of 1880-1905, and, most obviously, in the much imitated circular reading room. His untiring efforts improved the finances of the museum and secured a better staff structure and conditions of service. For a time he was even able to achieve the semblance of his most flamboyant claim—to make the British Museum Library the best in the world for each of the world's literary languages, save only for the national library most closely associated with that language.

Panizzi's greatest single asset as an administrator was his ability to make powerful friends and to use them to assist him achieve his purposes for the museum. His faults, which were as numerous as his virtues, included an uncertain temper and a tendency to bedevil smooth relationships by favouring some and persecuting others of his staff, often for no well formed reasons. His incurable weakness for political intrigue, which so nearly brought him to a violent end as a young man, continued to cause him trouble to the end of his life, often at the expense of his own and the museum's best interests.

As so often happens, following the departure of a strong individualistic figure from an organization, the museum continued to make strong progress for a time after Panizzi's retirement, being borne along perhaps by the strength of the tide he created; but gradually the influence died away and was not replaced by another of a strength even approaching comparison. After several generations of difficult times and rather formless administration the British Museum has, of recent years, showed signs of strong resurgence and gathering self confidence. The triumphant carrying through of a new printed catalogue in the early 1960's is, perhaps, the most notable sign of this resurgence, more than compensating for the debacle of the second attempt at a printed catalogue, which staggered along from 1930-1954 without ever promising to be successfully completed, and eventually was discontinued before the letter 'E' had been reached.

The first report of the Trustees of the British Museum to be published since the second world war appeared in 1967, and covers the years 1939-1966. It reveals much of the genesis of a new self confidence and spirit of innovation in the museum. It is to be hoped that the long drawn out wrangle over the location of the urgently needed new building does not disperse this atmosphere in frustration. Certainly the plain speaking of the trustees in their recent dealings with the government is encouraging, but six years after the passage of the British Museum Act 1963 little concrete progress has been achieved, due, in the main, to the vacillations of government and the tortuous nature of local as well as national politics.

The 1966 report provides considerable historical background, and the resurgence of the museum since 1945 is especially clearly demonstrated in the statistical section. Grants in aid for purchase for all departments of the museum totalled £20,000 in 1945 and there were 515 staff. In 1966-1967 purchase funds were £297,000 and there were 1,356 staff. The National Reference Library for Science and Invention comes in for special mention in the report.

The British Museum Act 1963 repeals all previous legislation, and in particular:

1 The composition of the Board of Trustees is altered and their number reduced to 25.

2 A report is to be produced every three years.

3 Powers are provided for the sale, exchange or gift of duplicates or other books published not earlier than 1850 if, thereby, the terms of bequests are not violated.

4 The Natural History Department is to have its own Board of Trustees.

The functions of the British Museum Library are currently under close scrutiny, with specific emphasis in this examination being placed upon closer integration with the national system of libraries. Another aspect of the operations of the library which is under examination is that (in common with the other major national collections—the National Lending Library for Science and Technology, the National Central Library and the Science Museum Library and several others) of the co-ordination and rationalisation of services. In October 1967 the Department of Education and Science set up a committee under the chairmanship of Dr F S Dainton to examine the problem of co-ordinating the major national collections. The evidence of the Library Association to that committee is presented in the *Library Association record* 70(6) June 1968 154-159. In the same issue of this journal, D T Richnell's ' The national library problem ' comments sourly upon the reasoning which allowed such a committee to be established without any representations of the interests of librarians. Richnell does then proceed, however, to draw up very sensible criteria for the fruitful co-ordination of the activities of such libraries of national significance.

THE LIBRARY OF CONGRESS

Established in 1800, although prior to this date Congress had used Benjamin Franklin's Library Company of Philadelphia for reference purposes. The library was totally destroyed by fire in 1814, and was re-established under its first full time librarian, George Watterson, with 6,000 volumes sold to Congress by President Jefferson. In 1816, by a liberal interpretation of the rules, the library was made available to scholars, and this interpretation has been the basis of all subsequent use by persons outside the members of Congress and their officers. Throughout the nineteenth century the appointment of Librarian to Congress was frequently the subject of political friction, at one time the post came almost to be recognised as a sinecure for a political journalist favourable to the government of the day.

As in the case of the British Museum, the origins of the present greatness of the library can be seen in the activities of a single individual, who was prepared to devote half a lifetime to the creation of a sound administrative structure. Though not so ebullient a character as Panizzi, the soundness of Ainsworth Spofford's administration from 1864-1897 is undoubted. During this period the nucleus of the magnificent research collections was brought together and new buildings provided which, it was intended, would cope with the growth of a century. After a two year interregnum following Spofford's death, Herbert Putnam was appointed librarian, following what was probably the sharpest and 'dirtiest' of the political wrangles which had characterised the appointment of librarian since it was established. Putnam came to the office of librarian from the post of Chief Librarian at Boston Public Library; he was the first 'career' librarian to hold the appointment. His reign lasted forty years, until 1939. His period of office built in spectacular fashion upon Spofford's foundation. The buildings which were to last a century were full before 1920, causing Putnam to secure two further extensions and, finally, an annexe larger in extent than all of the existing buildings together. In all, the collections increased tenfold during Putnam's forty years in office.

Putnam was a remarkably able administrator and an inspiring leader, with the gift of choosing capable subordinates and delegating fearlessly to them. The inception of the Library of Congress printed catalogue card scheme, the Library of Congress classification and the growth of a structure of subject specialists and eminent consultants all stem from the early years of Putnam's administration.

With Archibald McLeish, who held office from 1939-1944, Congress reverted to the appointment of a non-Librarian, in this case with great success. It was during McLeish's administration that the first tentative outlines of the Farmington Plan (see chapter eight) emerged. Dr Luther Evans, who held office from 1944-1953, having been promoted from the chief assistantship, left to become Director General of UNESCO. The eleventh Librarian of Congress, L Quincy Mumford (1953-), is the first library school trained person to hold the appointment.

The question of whether the Library of Congress should become the National Library of the USA in name and constitution is one which is currently receiving a great deal of examination. Paul Dunkin's 'Pyramid or volcano?' *Library journal* 88(1) Jan 1 1963 51-57 summarizes a colloquy between L Quincy Mumford and D J Bryant on this subject.

The services of the Library of Congress to the national system of libraries are extensive. In the *Annual report of the Librarian of Congress for the year ending June 30th 1962* (Washington, Government Printing Office, 1963), Dr Mumford claimed that 'The Library of Congress today performs more national library functions than any other national library in the world'. Among the most significant of these functions are the following, which are taken from the list of sixteen which he gave:

1 Services as a centre for co-operative cataloguing.

2 Publisher of the *National union catalog*.

3 The development and maintenance of a comprehensive general classification scheme.

4 The administration of a books-for-the-blind scheme.

5 Extensive research in library technology.

6 Participation in a nation-wide co-operative loans system.

John F Stearns has described the role of the Library of Congress in relation to inter-library co-operation in ' The national referral centre: a new service of the Library of Congress ' *Libri* 15(4) 353-359. This service was established with the assistance of the National Science Foundation as ' a clearing house to provide comprehensive and co-ordinated access to the nation's resources of scientific information '.

The drive to streamline and speed up the multifarious activities of the world's greatest library is made manifest in the report by G W King *et al Automation and the Library of Congress* (Council on Library Resources). The *Annual reports of the Librarian of Congress* are a useful source of information on the activities of the library and should be closely studied.

THE BIBLIOTHÈQUE NATIONALE

Like many of the European national libraries, the Bibliothèque Nationale evolved out of the collections of the royal house. Almost without exception, the kings of France were interested in book collection and their collections were always open to scholars. The Royal Library had many notable librarians—Bude, Colbert, the Bignons (as a family they held the senior posts in the library for almost a century) and Van Praet, who successfully steered both himself and the library through the Revolution, making an already good library the greatest of its time, and, indeed, one of the greatest of all time, through his collection of the best from the dissolved monasteries and from the libraries of exiled or executed aristocrats.

The fortunes of the library have waxed and waned frequently over the past 150 years, though seem to have been more often in decline than ascendant. The longest period of settled and dynamic administration was the incumbency of De Lisle, from 1874-1907, which was followed by a serious decline, particularly during and after the first world war. However, despite shortages of funds, considerable efforts were made to modernize the buildings and the routines in the inter-war years, though their effects were hardly felt before the second world war brought about a further recession in the library's fortunes, creating staff shortages and huge arrears of work only recently overcome. The Bibliothèque Nationale is currently enjoying something of a revival in its fortunes, but is a comparatively unknown quantity to English speaking librarians due to the lack of accessible readings.

THE NATIONAL LIBRARY OF SCOTLAND

The library, founded in 1682, was privately owned by the Faculty of Advocates until 1925, when it was taken over by the state and given its present name under the terms of the *National Library of Scotland Act 1925*. The history of the library and of the growth of its collections under various librarians, sometimes distinguished and often eccentric, is detailed in *National libraries of the world* (Library Association, second edition 1957) edited by F J Hill. A special article in the *Times literary supplement* for August 28 1953 is another valuable reading, as are the library's *Annual reports*.

The policy of the library is primarily the collection of the records of Scottish culture, but there exists the important secondary function of providing an internationally based research collection of a high quality for the benefit of Scottish scholars. The library is organised in two departments, Printed Books and Manuscripts. There is a stock of one and a half million volumes, impressively housed in new buildings opened in 1955.

THE NATIONAL LIBRARY OF WALES

At the national eisteddfod in 1873, the formation of a national collection of Welsh literature was proposed and approved. Almost immediately a start was made upon the collection of materials. The library received a Royal Charter in 1907, and in the same year the first Librarian, John (later Sir John) Ballinger, was appointed. He found a strong nucleus of materials for the library already available, based principally upon the bequests of Sir John Williams. Permanent buildings were commenced in 1911 on an impressive site on Aberystwyth, this location having been preferred to the counter-claims of Cardiff. The central block of the buildings was not completed until 1955, leaving storage areas and additional technical areas still to be added as opportunity offers. The library is organized into three departments, Printed Books, Manuscripts and Prints and Drawings. Fine collections of Irish and Scots Gaelic, Manx, Cornish and Breton literature are included, besides the massive Welsh materials. Like the National Library of Scotland, an important secondary objective is the provision of a high quality general research collection, and the library too enjoys legal deposit privilege.

The library was the first in Britain to be classified by the Library of Congress classification, and it produces an important annual national bibliography, *Bibliotheca Celtica*. Readings on the history of the library include an article in the *Times literary supplement* for July 10 1953, and another, by E D Jones, ' The National Library of Wales ' *Library world* 62(728) February 1961 177-181. The library itself publishes an *Annual report* and a descriptive pamphlet *The National Library of Wales: a brief summary of its history and activities*.

LEGAL DEPOSIT PROBLEMS AND FUNCTIONS

Long used as a means of enriching the collections of national libraries at minimal cost, legal deposit privileges owe their origins to the *Ordinance de Montpelier* 1537, which was the first regulation concerned with the practice. In some countries, legal deposit is used as a control in the censorship of the press (*eg* Japan); in others it is necessary in order to obtain the benefits of copyright protection.

Since legal deposit was first introduced into Britain there have been many variations of practice. Thomas Bodley, in reorganizing the moribund Oxford University Library, made a private arrangement with the Stationers Company to receive copies of all newly registered books. The Star Chamber decrees of 1637, which provided more firmly for the compulsory registration of books with the Stationers Company, *inter alia* strengthened the legal deposit position. *The Copyright Act* of 1709 provided regulations for the deposit of copies with nine libraries, and also gave rise to the frequent confusion between copyright protection and legal deposit —a point which has never been at issue in the British legislation. At the 1801 Act of Union with Ireland, eleven deposit copies were required for distribution to the same number of libraries, though in 1856 the number was reduced to five, at which figure it stayed until 1911 when the National Library of Wales was added.

Though unfavourably regarded by publishers as an unfair direct tax upon their enterprise, it is widely practised and some countries demand many more than the six copies required by British law. In some countries, however, deposit is voluntary, for example Switzerland. The arguments for and against the practice are summarized most ably by James Ollé in 'Free books in an affluent society' *Library world* 64(750) December 1962 162-167. R C B Partridge examines practice throughout the world in an article in T Landau's *Encyclopaedia of librarianship* (Bowes and Bowes, 1966).

Some of the questions which need to be asked about the practice of legal deposit with special reference to Britain are:

1 While it is undeniable that the practice is valuable as a means of accumulating the complete printed records of a nation's culture for the national library, is it really reasonable to extend the principle in addition to three (university) libraries (those of Oxford and Cambridge Universities and Trinity College Dublin)?

2 If so, should not certain designated regional public reference libraries be made beneficiaries, instead of the closed community university collections now receiving benefit?

3 Should a second copy not be available to the British Museum for international exchange purposes, as is the practice in some countries?

4 Should not the National Central Library have at least one copy to provide the nucleus of an inter-library co-operation collection?

5 Should not the practice of legal deposit be abolished, and the purchase funds of the depository libraries increased to enable them to purchase everything they need to have?

The International Federation of Library Associations survey of the state of the art of legal deposit, published in 1963 appeared in French, but has been generously summarized in English in *Library science abstracts* 13401. The survey indicated that twenty four of the twenty nine states in Europe had legal deposit regulations, and that throughout the world practice with regard to the number of copies which needed to be deposited varied from one to no less than forty four! The survey indicates that, properly enforced, legal deposit provides the best basis for securing the means to produce a definitive national bibliography.

There is an excellent section on legal deposit problems in *Five years work in librarianship 1961-1965* (Library Association, 1968) pp 11-12.

OTHER NATIONAL LIBRARIES: BRIEF NOTES ON SOME USEFUL SOURCES
With the British Museum, the Library of Congress and the Bibliothèque Nationale, as the really great national libraries of the world, must be ranked the Lenin Library in Moscow. In terms of sheer size, only the Library of Congress can compare with it. The degree of its integration into the national system of libraries has already been referred to. Readings are I Kondakov's 'The centenary of the Lenin State Library' UNESCO *Bulletin for libraries* 17(1) January-February 1963 25-26 and Jacob Miller's ' The Lenin Library' *Library review* (137) Spring 1961 26-29. The first reading concentrates upon the role of the library in relation to the national system of libraries; the second pays more attention to the nature of the collections, as, indeed, does an article in *Times literary supplement* (3057) June 29 1962 484.

The national libraries of the commonwealth countries provide interesting comparisons with those of the old world. Because of their relative youth, they have been able to benefit greatly from the experiences of the older national libraries. The National Library of Australia in Canberra is, naturally enough, the Parliamentary collection, but it has also taken upon itself many of the 'ideal' functions listed above. John Balnaves deals succinctly with its origins and activities in his book *Australian libraries* (Bingley, 1966), and H L White covers much the same ground in an article in *Australian library journal* 14(2) June 1965 56-60.

Canada was without a national library until 1946 but the effectiveness of its build up after so late a start is to be seen in W H Snape's ' The National Library of Canada' *Library world* 67(791) May 1966 319-324. Also relevant is *Canadian libraries* by H C Campbell (Bingley, 1969).

An Act of Parliament to establish the National Library of New Zealand was not passed until October 1965, and it is interesting to read of the reasons for the establishment of such a library in a country traditionally well served with good libraries already. ' The New Zealand National Library: the New Zealand Library Association submission' *New Zealand libraries* 21(4) June-July 1958 90-91, and S Perry's ' National Library: report of the Parliamentary Select Committee' *New Zealand libraries* 21(7) October 1958 137-141, provide the basic readings.

Carl M White's *The National Library of Nigeria: growth of the idea, problems and progress* (Lagos, The Federal Ministry of Information, 1964) is essential reading for those interested in the manifold problems and challenges of the establishment of national libraries in developing countries.

UNIVERSITY LIBRARIES: FUNCTIONS

The concept of the library as the ' soul ' of a university, the sun around which all teaching revolves, is widely acknowledged. As the University Grants Committee put it in their first annual report in 1921: ' The character and efficiency of a university may be gauged by its treatment of its central organ, the library. We regard the fullest provision for library maintenance as the primary and most vital need in the equipment of the university . . .' As L Jolley said in his important article ' The function of a university library' *Journal of documentation* 18(3) September 1962 133-142,

'If the UGC really believed that adequate libraries were the essential basis for a satisfactory university, for a very long time it took no steps to make them possible'. He does go on to say, however, that the position has changed somewhat, and that now we are beyond the stage of lip service to the ideal and into a time when responsible people in authority are making careful assessments of the nature of the essential functions of the university library.

The Association of University Teachers open their document *The university library* (AUT, 1964) with the bold statement ' The prime function of the university library is to provide facilities for study and research for the members of its own institution. At the same time, there is considerable support for the view that it should serve a wider circle of users and not adopt too restrictive an attitude which would be contrary to academic traditions '. The claim that this statement is ' bold ' arises out of the present situation in British university libraries; many are barely able to cope with the demands being made upon them by their own circle of users, let alone capable of opening their doors to others. The AUT do, however, emphasize from the beginning that such a wider conception of service would inevitably be conditional upon much larger amounts of money becoming available.

Arthur T Hamlin, in the introduction to an article 'The libraries of the universities of Italy' *Libri* 15(2) 1965 138-158, examines the functions of university libraries and concludes that conservation of knowledge is an important function of the university as a whole, and that it is through the university library that it carries this function through to its conclusion. With this as the primary function (a position agreed to by W L Guttsman in an article ' Learned librarians and the structure of academic libraries ' in the same issue of *Libri* 159-167) Hamlin mentions two other subsidiary purposes. These are: the extension of knowledge, carried out mainly through library co-operation; and the transmission of knowledge, which he feels can best be achieved by the encouragement of programmes of independent study by students who are thus obliged to use the library.

It is to the *Parry report* that one must look for a fully definitive treatment of the functions of the university library. In this source, the functions in relation to the undergraduate, the graduate, the scholar (sic!), the special collection and outside bodies, are examined separately.

In brief the report makes the following points about each: For the undergraduate teaching function, the call is for duplicate copies of certain key texts sufficient to enable the tutorial based upon independent study to flourish. Such a provision is expensive. For the graduate, the need is for a wide range of material, especially of the periodical and bibliographical type. This is also an expensive provision. For the scholar (by whom the report means post-doctoral research students and staff), demands are even heavier in respect of specialised material in a wide range. The *Parry report* mentions as an important point in respect of this type of provision, that the university library able to make really good collections available acts as a kind of ' bait ' to attract really able men to the university. As a repository for special collections the function of the library is to underline the need for the preservation of knowledge in all its forms. The composers of the *Parry report* did not look favourably upon the idea of the university library serving users outside the university—the ' public in general' as they called them. Thomas Parry summed up his impressions of the deliberations of his committee in a paper ' University libraries and the future ' *Library Association record* 70(9) September 1968 225-229.

Perhaps one of the most stimulating and thought provoking articles to appear on the subject of the functions of the university library is N W Beswick's ' The library-college—the true university ' *Library Association record* 69(6) June 1967 198-202. This is an account of an American concept in the building of a college around and within a library, with the bookstock utilised to the full by teachers who are also sound bibliographers.

THE HISTORY OF THE UNIVERSITY LIBRARY

Wherever students and scholars have gathered, so too have books. Evidence that the ancient Chinese learning centres, and the academies of ancient Greece, had large collections of books and that later on the great teaching monasteries placed great value on the use of libraries is examined by Harry J Vleeschauer in *Mousaion* (31, 32) 1958 under the title 'Academies and libraries', which traces the history of the idea of the university in relation to the growth of the collection of books. *Mousaion* is not the most easily accessible of sources, but *Library science abstracts* 9853 gives a useful summary of this very valuable historical survey.

Before 1800 there were only seven universities in the British Isles: Oxford (founded 1163), Cambridge (1209 ?), St. Andrews (1411), Glasgow (1453), Aberdeen (1494), Edinburgh (1582) and Trinity College Dublin (1591). The foundations of Durham University (1832) and London (1836) were simply a foretaste of the tremendous growth in the number of modern university foundations, especially since 1945, when a number of civic colleges emerged as full universities—Exeter, Leicester, Hull—and a large number of completely new establishments were formed. In point of total size, only three university libraries in the United Kingdom possess more than one million volumes—Oxford, Cambridge and London (and this last only achieves this size by counting together the many separate collections scattered around a very large campus). The two ancient English foundations deserve special mention on account of their antiquity and their richness of collections, but their size is, of course, in some measure due to the legal deposit privilege.

CAMBRIDGE UNIVERSITY LIBRARY

The origins of the library are obscure. A catalogue for the year 1424 listed 122 volumes in stock, and the rate of growth from this point was hardly meteoric; in 1473 there were 330 volumes, in 1528 600, and then a catalogue of 1556 indicated that the purges of the Reformation had reduced the stock to 175 volumes. Of this last figure some 130 volumes are still extant and in the library. Like the Bodleian library in Oxford, the library of Cambridge University does not have any specially notable historical events in the years down to about 1850 when the legal deposit privilege, properly enforced for the first time, began to cause swift growth. Henry Bradshaw, librarian from 1868-1886, and Francis Jenkinson, librarian from 1889-1923, did much between them to raise the library to its present eminence. Its handsome buildings, opened in 1934, are, however, somewhat off centre to be ideally sited. The early history of the library is dealt with by J C T Oates ' The Cambridge University Library' *Library quarterly* 32(4) October 1962 270-286, which also provides a bibliography of further useful sources for the study of the history of the library.

OXFORD UNIVERSITY LIBRARY

The early foundations at the Old Congregation House (1327), and at Duke Humfrey's Library (1435), were moribund by the turn of the sixteenth century. Duke Humfrey's Library was largely dispersed at the Reformation. The history of the university library must really date from Sir Thomas Bodley's re-foundation of Duke Humfrey's Library in 1600. An ex-diplomat with wide European connections and a scholarly bent, Bodley, with his librarian Thomas James (died 1629) made a vigorous start. Bodley's penchant for orientalia began a pattern which has produced in the Bodleian a strong collection, among the best in the world of its type.

Thomas Hyde, librarian from 1665-1701, and himself a distinguished orientalist, produced the first printed catalogue in 1674. Although there must have been some important occurrences in the history of the library in the eighteenth and early nineteenth centuries, they do not show up brightly in a reading of the history of the library, and it was only during the incumbency as librarian of the singularly named Bulkeley Bandinet, from 1813-1860, that distinctive progress began to be made. Bandinet was a most acquisitive librarian, who not only made legal deposit work properly, but used every other wile that an ingenious disposition could contrive to enrich the collections under his charge. Other notable librarians have been W B Nicholson, perhaps best remembered as the founding father of the Library Association, Falconer Madan (evocatively portrayed by Ernest Savage in his autobiography *A librarian's memories*) and Craster. It was this latter librarian who planned the new buildings for the Bodleian opened in 1946, and who produced the definitive history *History of the Bodleian Library 1845-1945* (OUP, 1952). The present-day organization of the library is described by J N L Myres ' The Bodleian Library' *Library world* 62(730) April 1961 225-229. There was a valuable article describing the richness of the collections in *Times literary supplement* September 24 1954.

Oxford colleges, perhaps to an even greater extent than their Cambridge counterparts, have some distinguished libraries in their own right—University College and Balliol are the earliest examples. Highly competent departmental (faculty) libraries are another feature of the very effective network of libraries serving the university.

OTHER BRITISH UNIVERSITIES

The major feature deserving of attention in the history of British university libraries is the tremendous rate of growth in the last ten to fifteen years, when compared with the sluggishness of their earlier years.

Really serious work on the general history of university libraries in the United Kingdom remains to be attempted, though E G Baxter's 'A preliminary historical survey of developments in university libraries in Great Britain' *Library Association record* 56 (9 & 10) September and October 1954 330-335, 389-393 cites eighty three sources which, taken together, cover much of the ground. George Chandler's *Libraries in the modern world* (Pergamon, 1965) and B S Page's 'University library developments' *Library Association proceedings, papers and summaries of discussions of the annual conference 1957* 52-58 provide helpful background. The feature 'University and research library notes', which appeared irregularly in the *Library Association record* for many years, provides a commentary on developments. Descriptions of individual libraries have frequently appeared in the professional press, and the following are a representative selection: 'University College Library' by Ruth Martin *Library world* 65(765) March 1964 296-298; a contribution by J H P Pafford 'The University of London Library' appeared in R Irwin and R Staveley's *The libraries of London* (Library Association, second revised edition 1964). P Sheldon's 'Hull University Library' in *The Yorkshire librarian* (30) September 1965 13-17 is a valuable survey of one of the newer foundations, which has the advantage not shared by many of the 'civic' universities of a tightly knit campus with the library beautifully sited in the middle; C P Finlayson and S M Simpson 'The Library of the University of Edinburgh: the early period 1580-1710' *Library history* 1(1) Spring 1967, and Moira Burgess's *Scottish libraries: triennial review* (Scottish Library Association, 1966) are two useful Scottish sources. The section on university libraries in *Five years work in librarianship 1961-1965* (Library Association, 1968) by P Havard Williams is a masterpiece of compression of, and sagacious comment on, a large number of references to the literature. The problems of the putative 'Open University' in relation to its library service were discussed at a conference in the west of England the papers of which are available from the Library

Association South Western Branch c/o County Library, Dorchester, Dorset.

Three papers of great value in providing an overview of the state of the art of university librarianship in this country appeared in *Librarianship in Britain today* (Library Association, 1967) edited by Professor W L Saunders of the Sheffield University postgraduate school of librarianship. They are ' British university librarianship in the Robbins era: the established universities ' by K W Humphreys, ' The newer universities ' by H Fairhurst, and ' Library developments in the new technological universities ' by A C Bubb.

UNIVERSITY LIBRARIES IN THE UNITED STATES OF AMERICA

The most striking feature of the history of university libraries in the USA has been the sheer speed of their build up. Harvard University Library (established 1636) had only 50,000 volumes in 1850 but over seven million in 1968; Yale has five million, and over forty other university libraries hold one million or more volumes. The statistics of sizes and growth rates of libraries are dazzling to British eyes. The most convenient source of such statistics is *Bowker annual* (New York, R R Bowker Inc). Size is no guarantee of quality, but nevertheless many American university libraries have contrived to obtain rich resources of early European background material to supplement the virtual saturation buying of modern material which is undertaken co-operatively. L R Wilson and M F Tauber's *The university library* (Columbia University Press, third edition 1964) is the most detailed account of the history and functions of the university library in the United States; the work is easily and widely accessible. E S Fox 'Academic libraries in the United States' *Library world* 68(799) January 1967 183-187, L M Morsch 'Academic and research libraries in the United States' in C M White's *Bases of modern librarianship* (Pergamon, 1964) pp 42-54, and Marietta Daniel's ' University libraries in the Americas: the inter-American seminar' *College and research libraries* 23(1) January 1962 28-32, are all further valuable sources of background.

OTHER COUNTRIES

R Vosper's ' European university libraries: current status and developments ' *Library trends* 12(4) April 1964 is a comprehensive record of the affairs of university libraries on the continent of Europe, including, among other countries, accounts of libraries in Belgium, Bulgaria, France, Germany and Austria. The somewhat curious structure of German university libraries (to British eyes at least)—their special status as state/public/university libraries with independent 'institute' libraries within the university, usually under the control of individual professors and completely independent from the main library—needs some study to appreciate fully. Similar patterns can be discerned in Austria and certain of the Scandinavian countries. References to the history, present status and future of German university libraries include the following: R Juchhoff ' The living tradition of the university and research libraries in Germany' *in* C M White's *Bases of modern librarianship* (Pergamon, 1964) pp 80-90, K Garside ' Reflections of a British university librarian on recent trends in Western Germany' *Libri* 16(1) 1966 10-17, and C Wehmer's 'The organization and origins of German university libraries'. *Library trends* 12(4) April 1964 491-512. The picture which such articles present is of libraries on closed access with little direct relationship to the teaching functions of the university, and this is sharply contrasted in Paul Kaegbein's description of ' The Technological University Library in Berlin' *Library Association record* 70(7) July 1968 174-176. In this library, reader services with direct relevance to the teaching role of the university are highly developed. Although the majority of the stock is on closed access, modern mechanical aids bring out the required items to readers quickly and efficiently.

Besides an article on French university libraries in the issue of *Library trends* mentioned above, Jean Bleton's 'New universities in France' UNESCO *Bulletin for libraries* 13(5-6) May-June 1959 115-119 is useful. Swedish university libraries are treated at length in a valuable booklet produced by the Swedish Institute, *Archives and libraries in Sweden*, and in K C Harrison's *Scandinavian libraries* (Deutsch, 1969), which also, of course, provides good general coverage of the other countries in the region, Norway, Finland, Denmark and Iceland. L Gronberg comments upon the problems raised by the combination of university and national library in the scandinavian countries in *Libri* 17(1) 1967 59-62.

L E Taylor's *South African libraries* (Bingley, 1967) is valuable for its copious reference to other sources, as well as for its summary of the history and present position of the libraries in South Africa. The development of university libraries and librarianship in South Africa (as one, formerly, of the commonwealth countries) is of interest to British librarians for comparative purposes, because of the common roots of many of the early librarians, who were expatriate Britons. The evolution of a library for the British 'Open University' makes Miss Taylor's brief reference to the all-correspondence-course South African University and its library of topical interest. S I Malan's 'University libraries in the Republic of South Africa' *Library world* 64(755) May 1963 324 is an accessible source of considerable value. Reuben Musiker, a deputy university librarian, contributes frequent articles to *South African libraries* on 'University progress in South Africa'.

COMMONWEALTH COUNTRIES

Harrison Bryan's *Australian university libraries: today and tomorrow* (Bingley, 1966) with John Balnaves *Australian libraries* (Bingley, 1966) are the obvious sources. The value of Balnaves' book lies particularly in his separate brief description of each university library. The University of Sydney Library is, by a considerable distance, the largest university library in Australia, with just over one million volumes. A feature of these libraries in Australia is that, typically, they serve student populations much larger than those in British universities of similar age. There is a tendency to dissipate resources over many departmental libraries, most of them inadequately staffed. D H Borchardt 'The University of Tasmania Library 1889-1959' *Australian library journal* 9(4) October 1960 165-170 refers to this point as a feature of this small library and indicates that in Australia, as elsewhere, it is a source of friction—he mentions a 'wrangle' over the question.

New Zealand libraries, the official organ of the New Zealand Library Association, is the obvious source for news on academic libraries in that country. F A Sandall's 'Tea for two: university libraries in New Zealand 1945-1959' *New Zealand libraries* 22(4) June 1959 77-88 contains some useful information, if the dialogue style of writing can be tolerated.

D H Varley's report of the 'Conference of university libraries in Tropical Africa' UNESCO *Bulletin for libraries* 19(2) March-

April 1965 73-76 illustrates the dynamic growth which has taken place in Africa south of the Sahara. Such growth was often prompted by the presence of advisers from Commonwealth countries, or from the United States, and still relies heavily upon expatriate librarians from these countries for senior staff provision.

COLLEGES OF FURTHER EDUCATION LIBRARIES

Two books of note examining the status of such libraries have appeared in recent years. D L Smith and E G Baxter's *College library administration in colleges of technology, art, commerce and further education* (OUP, 1965) and G H Wright's *The library in colleges of commerce and technology* (Deutch, 1966). Smith and Baxter open their book in a way which dramatizes the function of a further education college library in somewhat strange contrast to the rather abstract, philosophical terms used in the *Parry report's* discussion of the functions of a university library. Their introduction describes the lunchtime scene in a college library as one of intense activity, centred strongly around the librarian on duty. Without actually saying so in so many words, Smith and Baxter clearly regard the function of such a library as the provision of a highly personal service to both staff and students alike—the librarian, in their terms, is guide, philosopher and friend to students and their tutors working in an enormous range of subject fields and at many different intellectual levels.

Properly organized college libraries are of relatively recent origin. As recently as 1954, only 160 out of 555 further education college libraries had more than 300 volumes, and in only fifty two were there qualified librarians. Progress in the development of adequate library services was led throughout the non-university sector during the 1960's by the libraries of the Colleges of Advanced Technology, which ultimately advanced to full university status as a consequence of the government report *Higher education: report of the committee appointed by the prime minister under the chairmanship of Lord Robbins 1961-1963* (HMSO cmnd 2154: 1963), more familiarly known as the *Robbins report*. The degree to which it has been found necessary to increase the financial resources of the former colleges of advanced technology following the up grading to University status has been one indication of the shortcomings of the library provision in all libraries in the non-university teaching sector. The transition into universities did, however, leave the non-university sector in some danger of losing its whole leadership.

The *Robbins report* created the conditions for the emergence of another sector of leadership within the further education field, however, by its reference to the need for the larger colleges in the local authority sphere of control to conduct degree and higher degree work on an increasing scale. Already such colleges were undertaking some degree level work, under arrangements with the external department of the University of London or, less commonly, in association with local universities—for example at the colleges of technology at Belfast and Sunderland. The *Robbins report* recommended the establishment of a body which would enable colleges to devise and operate courses for degrees of their own choosing. The Council for National Academic Awards (CNAA) was the result, and it was established in 1964 with a Royal Charter allowing it to grant degrees. In essence, the function of CNAA is to inspect proposals for degree courses devised by colleges at the first and higher degree level, and, following a rigorous inspection of the physical and academic environment of the college, to grant permission for proposals which meet the high standards of CNAA to be operated as degree studies. It is to the great credit of CNAA that, from the beginning, they placed due emphasis upon the need for colleges aspiring to their degrees to maintain a high standard of library provision. In several instances colleges have had their submissions rejected or delayed pending improvements in their library provision. Such a practice has had a signal effect upon the standards of provision for libraries, and in some places has helped to produce standards of service only a little lower than those enjoyed by universities.

Another event with an impact upon library provision in colleges followed quickly after the CNAA establishment. This was a government proposal to establish a number of 'super-colleges' in the further education sector. The government 'white paper' *A plan for polytechnics and other colleges* (HMSO cmnd 3006: 1966) introduced the concept of colleges whose principal aim was to be the provision of courses at about the first degree level, with a strong vocational flavour, closely integrated with local industry and commerce for full time, part time and 'sandwich' course students. While a leavening of research work was to be expected, this was not to be a 'primary' purpose of these new institutions, which were formed from mergers of some of the most outstanding of the higher level further education colleges in the country. One of the aims of the plan was to concentrate the higher level, and therefore more expensive, work into a small number of large institutions. The first thirty polytechnics to be designated include some of the colleges which might, in different circumstances, have become full universities in their own right. Some of the polytechnics designated are simply up-gradings of single colleges, for instance in the case of Constantine College of Technology in Middlesbrough. Others were amalgamations of several existing colleges of relatively small size, which, when combined, form sizeable units, for instance in Leeds where four colleges became merged into one. Where the polytechnic arises out of one of the single college units, library development can go on uninterrupted and with few new problems. Where, however, the polytechnic is an amalgam of several colleges on sites separated by up to twenty miles the inevitable result is organizational problems which are as severely felt in respect of the library as in any other aspect of their work.

'Libraries in the new polytechnics: a guide to planning requirements' *Library Association record* 70(9) September 1968 240-243 is a document approved by the Library Association Council in June 1968. It summarizes the functions envisaged for the polytechnic library and is a valuable contribution to the literature, despite such monuments to pedestrianism in prose as 'the library should play a central role in the educational programme as a major teaching instrument'. The document envisages a basic stock of 150,000 volumes and 3,000 periodical titles to serve the minimum of 2,000 students planned for each polytechnic. This minimum standard document is a welcome one, especially in terms as generous as this. Too often in the past the Library Association minimum standards have tended to be a conservative embarrassment to the more progressive libraries. No polytechnic library reaches anywhere near this projected level of service as yet. Indeed one of the major problems facing the new polytechnics is that their standards of library service now fall far short of the ideal, even in the basic bibliography, let alone in the range and depth of their subject coverage. The educational development of the polytechnics will certainly not stand still over the next ten years to allow their libraries to catch up with the minimum standards proposed. They will develop their enterprise in every direction, and probably most significantly relative to the present position in the arts and social sciences fields. Unless infusions of money at a much higher rate than hitherto are put into the polytechnic libraries they will be as inadequate in ten years time as they are, in most cases now.

P H Sewell says, in a stimulating article ' The development of technical college libraries ' *Library world* 68(804) June 1967 331-333, ' The level of their work and the academic status of the colleges themselves will make major developments (*ie* in libraries) essential '. Where will the money for these ' major developments ' come from, however? The University Grants Committee made an initial grant of some £175,000 to new university libraries and, miserably inadequate though this has ultimately proved to be, it looks like a vision of another world to the polytechnic libraries.

The creation of the polytechnics, like the creation of the colleges of advanced technology before them, puts most of the front runners into a special category clearly designed for differential treatment, leaving behind lesser colleges who will need, yet again, to look for their leadership. This apparently inevitable process of creaming off the higher level work into a small number of colleges every few years must lead to difficulties, since the colleges so creamed off need to adjust their ideas to new demands, while the lesser colleges need to re-assess their standards of provision for their, usually, changed role.

Even with the creation of polytechnics, the non-polytechnic colleges will probably retain some of their higher level work. While the polytechnics will take some comfort from the fact that the level of their work is homogeneous in character, the lesser colleges will still find their basic problem to be the wide spread of levels of provision that they are expected to cater for. As D L Smith says in ' Technical future ' *Times educational supplement* March 11 1966, ' levels of attainment are quite extraordinarily uneven . . . from super-school to micro-university '.

The functions of technical college libraries: In their book mentioned above, Smith and Baxter give (pp 9-12) as the functions of the college library the following (summarized severely here):

1 Books etc to assist in passing examinations.

2 A selection of general reading to encourage students to widen their outlook—current affairs, literature, biography etc. (As the

authors rightly say, the larger libraries will solve this problem to a greater extent by the very range of the necessary provision to cope with the first point.)

3 Quick reference and factual material.

4 Provision for the development of staff interests, this involving the provision of much material of a higher standard than that strictly required for the needs of the college teaching activities.

5 The library must provide facilities for private study.

6 In some areas the technical college library should provide a technical information centre for the use of local industry, with the possibility of being able to call upon the specialist lecturing staff for assistance in amplifying the resources of the library itself.

The Association of Technical Teachers (ATTI) has issued a policy statement on the *Use of libraries* (ATTI, 1966). In the second paragraph of this statement their attitude to the library becomes clear when they say ' this report looks primarily at the college library as an essential part of technical teaching, and discusses how suitable instruction in the use of the library may be given to college students '. This view of the library as a teaching instrument echoes the terms of the Library Association in their polytechnic document mentioned above, and the policy statement further amplifies its meaning by the provision of many examples of the kinds of teaching programmes being carried out in technical college libraries. The theme is taken also by A J Aldous in his article ' Developing the small college library ' *Library world* 67 (789) March 1966 253-256. However, a letter to CTFE *Bulletin* (47) page 5 (the bulletin of the Library Association's Colleges of Technology and Further Education Sub-section) by J R A Walker deplores the emphasis placed upon teaching the use of the library, especially in so far as it leads to the designation of librarians as ' tutor-librarians '. This is a point which will be returned to in chapter four.

COLLEGES OF EDUCATION

At the time of publication of the first edition of this book, the three year course of teacher training was the norm, having then been quite recently introduced. The four year programme leading to a bachelor of education degree, though foreshadowed by the *Robbins report*, had not yet begun. Growth in the colleges of education over the last five years has been considerable. The

Parry report draws attention to the fact that the colleges of education were mainly of the 200-300 student size in 1960, but also to the fact that they have grown considerably since that time. Colleges of 750 students and above are quite common, while the largest, that at Jordanhill, Glasgow, has over 3,000.

The publication of *Library practice in colleges of education* (Library Association, 1966), edited by Norman Furlong, brought to a successful conclusion five years of work by a special committee of the, then, Training Colleges and Institutes of Education Subsection of the Library Association's University and Research Section. The work has a useful piece on the functions of the college of education library, on pages 16-18. *College of education libraries: recommended standards for their development* (Library Association/Association of Teachers in Colleges and Departments of Education, 1967) begins with a section on the functions of a college of education library, which indicates how difficult a job is the formulation of such a library: 'At a college of education students follow a course with two complementary and interrelated aspects; academic subjects, corresponding to fields of study in university faculties, and a range of vocational studies appropriate to teachers in training . . . the library must therefore be both a comprehensive general and academic library, and a professional library for prospective teachers, where all aspects of education and children's interests, including textbooks, audio-visual aids and children's books, are amply represented'. Nine specific functions of the library are then listed.

Accounts of the history and growth of particular college libraries are to be found in *Education libraries bulletin*, a lively periodical issued once a term from the Institute of Education, London University. *Five years work in librarianship* (Library Association, 1950-), issued every five years, contains material on college of education libraries. In the 1961-1965 volume there is a section by W H Shercliff which, besides reviewing British practice comprehensively, also covers Commonwealth and United States libraries of a similar kind. The Colleges, Institutes and Schools Sub-section of the Library Association's University and Research Section produces an excellent *Newsletter*, containing much discussion of the live issues in this fast growing sector of librarianship.

CHAPTER TWO : GOVERNMENT FINANCE AND ORGANIZATION

NATIONAL LIBRARIES: It is almost an invariable practice that the ultimate control of national libraries rests with a government department responsible for education and/or culture. What is curious, given this situation, is the number of instances in which the staffs of national libraries are granted conditions of service and scales of salary significantly below those offered to civil servants generally. Panizzi in Britain and Putnam in the United States both had battles to fight on this front, which, in the case of Britain at least, have hardly yet been entirely won. There follows a summary of the present pattern of organization of four national libraries, and then a more general statement of the common organizational arrangements of other national libraries.

The British Museum is administered under the terms of the *British Museum Act 1963* which has reduced the size of the governing body (called the trustees) to twenty five. It has also thereby strengthened its executive powers, for prior to the 1963 Act this body was large and amorphous, and had represented upon it descendants of the more notable benefactors, whose present day usefulness was sometimes questionable. As indicated in chapter one, the new trustees have the power to enter the institution more fully into the national system of libraries, to buy, sell or loan material under certain limitations, and to negotiate for the purchase of land for the benefit of the museum's further development.

The British Museum is administered by a Director and Principal Librarian who has always, hitherto, been appointed internally from the staff of the library. The open advertisement for the post in 1968 created a precedent which underlined to the world a determination on the part of the trustees to re-shape the museum's role. The library section of the museum is in the charge of the Principal Keeper of Printed Books with two keepers as his assistants, and a third in charge of the National Reference Library for Science and Invention. The Department of Manuscripts is in the charge of a keeper, as is the Department of Orientalia. The total professional staff of the library exceeds 300, all of whom are appointed by the Civil Service Commission.

The National Library of Scotland is governed by a board of trustees appointed under the terms of the *National Library of Scotland Act 1925*. The composition of the board represents, in part at least, the origins of the library, through the fact that a proportion of its members are representatives of the Faculty of Advocates, who owned the library from its inception in 1682 until 1925. The other representatives include persons appointed by the Scottish universities, local government authorities and the Crown. The National Library of Wales is similarly governed under the terms of the *National Library of Wales Act 1911*. There is a court of governors consisting of a president, vice-president, treasurer and appointees from the Privy Council, from universities and colleges in Wales, local authorities, lords lieutenant and sheriffs, and the thirty five Welsh members of parliament. There are also representatives of the various benefactors of the library, and a number of co-opted members. Because such a body would obviously be unwieldy for the day to day administration of affairs, there is an executive council of thirty three members and a separate finance committee.

The government of the Library of Congress is unique. As the library is still, by definition, the working library of the two houses of Congress, it is governed by a joint committee of both houses, though the librarian has very wide executive powers in his own right. He is a direct appointee of the President of the USA, and he is responsible directly to the Senate, without any department of state intervening on matters such as his budget. Staff appointments are made directly to the library, and are not regarded as part of the structure of the American civil service.

The organization of national libraries: The traditional pattern of organization is into sections according to the type of material being dealt with—books, manuscripts, maps, music etc. It is this kind of approach which is practised at the British Museum and the other British national libraries. The subject divisional plan, allowing as it does the integration of all types of library material irrespective of form into units, is seen by the late director, Sir Frank Francis, as the nearest possible approach to the ideal national library situation (*see National libraries: their problems and prospects* (UNESCO, 1960) pp 21-26). Sir Frank maintains further that the divisional plan leads to greater satisfaction for both staff and readers, due to the greater realisation of the potential for intensive service in depth which such a pattern allows.

Despite the increased demands on buildings and staff, the subject divisional plan seems to be inevitable for the well organized large library. It is significant, perhaps, that both of the libraries which are candidates for the title of the world's greatest —the Library of Congress and the Lenin Library in Moscow—are so organized. The principal problem for anyone who has not been able to see or work in one of the really large libraries is to appreciate the scale of the operations therein. An excellent impression of this scale is given by R D Rogers ' Administration of a giant . . .' *Library journal* 90(18) October 15 1965, which is an account of the activities of the Library of Congress.

National library finance: Whether it be the Library of Congress or the newest, smallest or least ambitious national library elsewhere which is being examined, the organization of their finances is probably broadly similar. One of the clearest ways to understand the sociological concept of the ' succession of goals ' is to examine the history of the development of a national library. The concept postulates that the achievement of goals only discloses further desirable goals to be achieved, which soon in turn come to be seen as basic. In the national library situation, the better the library service offered, the greater pressure there is to improve it, and the greater also the need to improve it, to keep pace with the demands made upon it. No librarian ever feels that he has enough money to develop his enterprise to its fullest extent, but national libraries have undoubtedly suffered more than most types from a shortfall of finance to develop the services demanded of them.

Funds for the support of national libraries usually come from the government in direct appropriations or grants in aid. Endowment funds rarely contribute significantly to the total of funds available for their administration—the Library of Congress receives about six percent of its total annual budgets from such a source, the National Library of Scotland three percent. Special purchases of books and equipment are sometimes aided by the existence of organizations of 'friends of the library'. There is, for example, a British organization 'Friends of National Libraries'. Gifts, bequests and public appeals can make a significant contribution to capital accounts on the financial side, and to the enrichment of the collections, especially when the gifts take the form, as they often do, of library materials. The national libraries of Scotland and Wales owe virtually all of their magnificent buildings to the generosity of private benefactors. The appeal to charity or cupidity, it must not be forgotten, has a long history as a means of endowing libraries; the British Museum's foundation was largely financed by a national lottery.

Technical services in national libraries: The studies made of the evolution of cybernetic aids to management and process control, coupled with the increasingly difficult tasks of bibliographical control in national libraries, due to the vast bulk and diversity of their accessions, has made it almost inevitable that such aids should also be called into service in the national libraries of the world. Equally inevitably, perhaps, it was in the Library of Congress that the lead in this new sphere was taken when, in 1961, the office of Information Systems Specialist was set up to study the applications of computers and other automated aids to the operations of the library. The Council on Library Resources made a $100,000 grant to the Library of Congress to survey the problems faced in automating the library. The report of the surveyors *Automation and the Library of Congress* (Washington, GPO, 1964) was summarized in *College and research libraries* 25(2) May 1964 120. Initially it is in the field of bibliographic control that the Library of Congress is channelling its efforts, with the aim of improving the 'point of sale' service to readers; but ultimately the necessity of redesigning the whole philosophy of the organization will need to be faced, so that the library will operate around a computer, with all of its systems tailor-made for the new situation, rather than being simply grafted on to the existing situation.

Cataloguing in national libraries: The concept of the national library operating the centralized cataloguing system for the whole country is increasingly encountered. The Library of Congress, once again, provides the pre-eminent example of this practice, though many other national libraries have followed suit, for instance in Japan and in Finland. The development of printed catalogues in volume form also owes much to the *Library of Congress catalog* (later the *National union catalog*), which began to be produced in 1942, using a technique of photographing rows of printed catalogue cards and making them up into page form entries by optical reduction, then printing by photolitho-offset. This technique, now much refined, is the one which enabled a triumphant job to be made of printing out the British Museum catalogue between the years 1959 and 1966. The National Library of Scotland is now also known to be interested in the possibility of reproducing its catalogues in this way.

Classification in national libraries: Classification, as a means of arranging national library collections, as opposed to arrangement by fixed location, is a moot point with national libraries, as with any other library of large size which is on closed access (most national libraries are). When large parts of collections are on open shelves available to the public directly, then classification is obviously desirable. On the other hand, it is questionable how far really large collections are susceptible to efficient browsing—which is something classification assists. The need to cater for potential expansion at any point in the shelving arrangements in a classified library implies the availability of large amounts of space to arrange books on the shelves with a good deal of space left idle for future expansion. But large amounts of space are rarely available for non-use in large libraries, and fixed location as a means of arrangement does enable the available space to be most efficiently used, since it is not necessary to leave room for expansion at any point in the arrangement, but simply to have enough space available at the end of the run of shelving to accommodate new accessions. Most national libraries work on closed access arrangements for the bulk of their stocks; some classify only their special collections or more recent accessions closely. Other libraries make full use of the facility for compact storage which fixed shelf location arrangements allow, and cannot, of course, allow readers direct access to shelves.

In circumstances such as those indicated above, the need for efficient catalogues needs no underlining, but it is a sad fact that most of the world's national libraries have serious arrears of cataloguing, which render recent accessions virtually useless to them. Even the Library of Congress has been obliged to make some use of fixed location, despite having perhaps the most efficient cataloguing organization of any national library. Its problem is to make the most efficient use of space, rather than to combat arrears of cataloguing. Nowhere, apparently, can the vicious circle of inadequate staff, poor provision of storage areas and burgeoning bibliographical control problems be escaped by traditional means. Both intellectually and in terms of capital investment, the problems of applying cybernation to bibliographic control are formidable, but this means represents the only real hope for large libraries ever to solve their most pressing problems. It has been suggested that the only means of carrying through the necessary programmes is by co-operation between a nation's libraries, as mooted by F J Hill in his chapter 'National libraries' *in Five years work in librarianship 1961-1965* (Library Association, 1968) p 21. The problems seem even larger than that, however, and will probably demand international co-operative effort in due course between the great libraries of the world.

UNIVERSITY LIBRARIES

Government: Full understanding of the pattern of government of a university library demands an appreciation of the way in which the university itself is governed, and the manner in which it is affected by influences from outside. The major outside influence, of course, is that which controls the purse strings. In the United Kingdom it is the University Grants Committee which controls university expenditure to a very large extent. The committee's quinquennial reports, presented to parliament as command papers, are a mine of information. *University development 1957-1962* (HMSO, cmnd 2267, 1964) traces the origins and development of the university pattern in Britain in chapter IV, where it summarizes the main outlines of their internal government. More importantly, perhaps, in chapter VIII is described the role of the committee and the working of its quinquennial system of grants. The report for the quinquennium 1962-1967 under the same title was published in November 1968. It was the University Grants Committee which was responsible for the commissioning and subsequent publication of the deliberations of the Committee on

Libraries, whose report, entitled *Report of the Committee on Libraries* (HMSO, 1967), is popularly known as the *Parry report*. The report has already had a far reaching effect upon the thinking of the University Grants Committee, and the controllers of the individual university libraries, and will have a long lasting value as a source document for students of the problems of the university libraries.

Fears that British universities are losing much of their traditional freedom of action in the conduct of their internal affairs have been frequently expressed in recent years. The increasing tendency of the government of the day to take unilateral action to control the activities of the universities in ways which accord with the political thinking of a particular Administration is regarded by many academics as a sinister turn of events. The details of the way in which the University Grants Committee derives its finance and administers it will be dealt with in the next section. In a situation such as that which, theoretically, obtained until recently, the universities derived their subsistence from general and special grants provided by the University Grants Committee, and, within fairly broad limits, the individual university could exercise a great deal of discretion over the use of the money granted. However, with the greatly increased financial demands made by the universities in recent years, the call for more direct control of the manner in which the universities disburse the taxpayers' money has become more and more insistent. Within the last two years the government has required that the accounts of individual universities be opened to the scrutiny of the Comptroller and Auditor-General. In other ways the government has made direct interventions in the internal affairs of universities, rather than, as traditionally was the case, dealing through the University Grants Committee. The result is that the credibility of the University Grants Committee, as a kind of ' buffer ' between the government and the universities, has become rather strained. There are university administrators who now regard the University Grants Committee as little more than a voice of the Department of Education and Science in the articulation of government policy to the universities, and this is indicated by Peter Scott's article ' Declining status of the UGC, independence lost to government ' *Times educational supplement* (2790) November 8 1968 1,023. It should be stated, however, that not all educationalists, and particularly not those responsible for the growth of the polytechnics, regard the measures to bring the universities under closer financial control as totally abhorrent.

The stresses and strains of the internal politics of universities are well documented in W B Palmer's 'University government and organization' in *British universities annual 1966* (The Association of University Teachers, 1967) 128-142. Amongst the problems dealt with are the difficulties arising out of the distortions of government, occasioned by the way in which universities are still struggling along with constitutions which were designed for the days when they had less than a thousand students and a hundred staff. Nowadays, many can boast up to seven times those numbers. E W Hughes presents an indication of how constitutions might be shaped in his pamphlet *The internal government of universities* (The Association of University Teachers, 1965). This pamphlet describes in particular the practices of the University of Newcastle.

Comparative information upon the status of universities in the various countries of the world is interestingly presented by Anthony Kerr's *The universities of Europe* (Westminster, Maryland, The Canterbury Press, 1962). For no very apparent reason, this text contains an appendix on the functions and organization of the University Grants Committee which is useful.

Specific descriptions of the role of the library in the life of the university are given by the *Parry report,* chapter eleven, where note is taken of the way in which the library is related to the governing body of the university. *The university library* (Association of University Teachers, 1964) presents the evidence submitted to the UGC Committee on Libraries, and it opens with the unequivocal statement that 'The prime function of the university library is to provide facilities for study and research for the members of its own institution'. The statement does go on, however, to explore the possibilities of a wider service to the community outside.

In British universities, the library is usually controlled through a committee of the senate. As paragraph 554 of the *Parry report* puts it 'The university library committee (with a variety of names) is most commonly a senate committee, although in a few universities it is a joint committee of the senate and the council. It may be composed of representatives of the faculties (and often appointed by them), with *ex officio* membership of the vice-chancellor, his deputy and some other officer of the university—the treasurer, bursar, secretary or registrar— who may be invited to attend only. The vice-chancellor is usually chairman and the librarian or registrar is the secretary of the committee.' The report also suggested that the universities should make arrangements to have the students represented upon the library committee.

In the United States, the pattern of government varies considerably. Sometimes the librarian is responsible only to the university president, while in other circumstances he may be responsible primarily to a committee of the main governing body of the university, or to a specially constituted board of trustees. The far reaching differences in the patterns of administration of the British, as compared with the European university library, are stressed by an Austrian librarian, Franz Kroller, in his article ' On the administration of English university libraries ' *Biblos* 11(4) 1962 211-221. The article is in German, but there is a long informative abstract available in English in *Library science abstracts* 12873. Among other points brought out in the article is that, already mentioned earlier, of the constitutional separateness of the Austrian university library from the university itself—a pattern repeated in many countries.

University library finance: University funds drawn from government sources are allocated on the recommendation of the University Grants Committee in quinquennial cycles. The procedure whereby this is done is fully described in paragraphs 586-597 of the University Grants Committee report *University development 1957-1962* (HMSO, cmnd 2267, 1964). Estimates are prepared by universities in the form prescribed by the University Grants Committee, who then make visitations to the individual universities to discuss the plans of the staff for the development of the university in the light of their submitted estimates. The visitations serve other useful subsidiary purposes, however. They enable the University Grants Committee to keep up to date with university thinking ' on site ', as it were. They give at least some members of the university staffs the opportunity to discuss the problems of university administration against the background of the national education picture, in such a way as to benefit both parties.

It is claimed that the quinquennial system enables the universities to think deeply about forward policy; indeed, it obliges them to do so. It is claimed that the quinquennial system guards against the possibilities of wild fluctuations in financial policy which might be attendant upon annual budgeting policies, and which would thus render long term planning difficult. On the other hand, if the beginning of a quinquennium happens to fall in particularly hard economic times, then a great deal of difficulty can arise, especially in capital works policy.

Once the quinquennial budget is settled by the University Grants Committee, acting in consultation with the Treasury, the university library can take steps to allocate its own funds. The practice of dividing funds into a general purpose fund and a periodical fund and then further dividing into departments, while it is still used, has now given way in most universities to a situation in which all funds are held centrally and purchases made solely at the discretion of the librarian, advised by academic and other staff. The principal reason for this change in recent years is that purchase funds, whilst not lavish, are much improved upon earlier levels and most libraries are able to provide every department with enough material at least for basic needs.

Chapter XII of the *Parry report* provides very detailed figures on university library finance. Among other things, it indicates that the percentage of total university expenditure available to the library has been consistently of the order of four percent since 1949. Examination of the University Grants Committee returns for a specific year indicate, however, that the average conceals one or two significantly higher percentages for individual universities—as high as 8·9 percent in one case, but also an appreciable number which are much lower, as low as two percent in one case. According to J W Scott's ' Value for money in university libraries ' *Library world* 65(768) June 1964 387-389, about half the total university library funds are appropriated for staff salaries and wages. The *Parry report* provides figures for library expenditure divided by the number of students, and arrives at the figure of £31 per student as the average, with a range of expenditures from £54 to £18 in individual universities. The number of books per head of the student population which are available ranges from 344 down to seventy with an average figure of 150.

Private endowments do not make as significant a contribution to the funds of university libraries in Britain as they do in so many universities in the United States. ' Extra-university sources of financial support for libraries: a symposium ' *College and research libraries* 23(6) November 1962 509-521 indicates the scale upon which some United States university libraries are privately supported, by revealing that there are eighteen universities which have an average of seven percent of their funds derived from endowments and donations—according to the results of a survey which this article reports. In Britain not more than two university libraries can approach such a figure. Some American libraries have associations of friends, according to S L Wallace ' *Friends of the library organization and activities* ' (ALA, 1962). B E Powell comprehensively reviews ' Sources of support for libraries in American universities' *in* J D Marshall's *The library in the university* (Shoestring, 1967).

With more and more government sponsored research being carried out in universities, the question arises whether the contracts ordering the research should include a clause making an allowance for financial provision for the library; it is not one which has been much aired in Britain. In the United States, where the scale of such work is altogether larger, some thought has been given to the problem, as will be seen from D C Weber's ' Library overhead allowances under government research agreements' *College and research libraries* 26(6) November 1965 490-492. A number of references to earlier literature on the subject are provided by R H Lagsdon in his ' Indirect costs of library services under US research agreements ' *College and research libraries* 23(1) January 1962 24-27.

A full consideration of the financial control of university libraries must include some reference to the problem of insurance of the collections and the buildings. It is probable that the university will have a comprehensive policy covering damage or destruction of buildings and their contents, but it behoves a librarian to be sure that the cover for the contents of a library is adequate. Nobody but an expert librarian is likely to have a realistic idea of the insurance cover necessary for collections of books. A non-expert will almost certainly undervalue such collections. The Library Technology Project of the American Library Association includes an item edited by E M Johnson *Protecting the library and its resources: a guide to physical protection and insurance* (American Library Association, 1963. LTP publication no 7).

The organization and administration of university libraries: The most difficult organizational problem for the university library is to decide to what extent pressures to provide a decentralized service through departmental libraries should be accepted. The problems solved, and those created by a decentralized structure of university libraries are discussed later in this book in chapter six. The German and Scandinavian models of 'institute' libraries are particularly relevant to such a discussion, as are the presence of college libraries which are separated from the main library structure in certain British universities.

The loans policy of university libraries and the hours of opening are, to some extent, linked questions. British and American university libraries are often praised for their liberal loans policy, and for the extent to which they are willing to allow totally open access to the bulk of theirs shelves. University libraries in many European countries are similarly prepared to adopt a liberal policy for loans, but very often unwilling, and indeed unequipped, to allow access to their shelves. Opening hours of British university libraries are beginning to reach realistic levels—realistic, that is, in relation to the demands made upon them. Eighty hours a week is now quite common in Britain, though in the United States a hundred hours plus is not unknown. Shortage of staff is one of the principal barriers to the provision of longer opening hours, and this is a disability which British university libraries are only slowly overcoming.

In circumstances in which opening hours must be restricted to a level lower than that demanded, a liberal policy for loans is a necessity. Wholesale loans, however, create considerable difficulty. A single person can monopolize a much sought-after volume for a long time. He is unlikely in the course of a loan to make such intensive use of a borrowed volume as could be made of that same volume in the university library by several people using it for reference there. It is significant of the problems and frustrations of students in finding wanted material in libraries that the burden of the National Union of Students evidence to the Committee on Libraries was that there was a need for longer hours of opening for university libraries, with a severe restriction upon loan facilities as a corollary.

Automation in university libraries: An organizational problem of growing significance concerns the effective use of the potentialities of the computer and other automated aids. Some of the early essays in this field are dealt with by A C Foskett's contribution to *Five years work in librarianship 1961-1965* (Library Association, 1968).

To a great extent existing schemes of automation based upon the computer have been concerned with attempts to solve various pressing problems of housekeeping routines, and the replacement of scarce clerical staff. An appreciation of the nature of the projects so far undertaken in British university and college libraries can be obtained by reference to the issues of *Program: news of computers in British university libraries* Volume 1 number 1 March 1966. John Harrison and Peter Laslett were responsible for the editing of the *Brasenose Conference on the automation of libraries* (Mansell Information, 1967); the main points of this conference were also summarized in UNESCO *Bulletin for libraries* 22(1) January-February 1968. These papers demonstrate how far the thinking on automation has progressed in British university libraries. They indicate a partial approach, with the application of automation being made to individual processes or groups of related processes. As Dr John Rose says in his *Automation: its uses and consequences* (Oliver & Boyd, 1967) such a partial approach, which regards the computer as little more than an extra office machine, albeit an extremely sophisticated one, is a negation of the real potential of these machines. To derive the maximum benefits from their use it is necessary completely to rethink the philosophy of an organization, in order to fit it to the computer, rather than to attempt to fit the computer to aspects of the existing organization. To do anything else, according to Rose, is to make very uneconomic use of very expensive equipment. Paul Wasserman's *The librarian and the machine* (Gale Research, 1965) is sub-titled ' Observations on the applications of machines in adminstration of college and university libraries '; it provides a very readable summary of the various potential applications of computers, and, like Rose, seems to indicate the folly of partial application. One very useful point which emerges from the book indicates the value of exercises in the application of computers to library situations, in forcing reappraisals of the aims and objectives of library services.

Classification and cataloguing in university libraries: The choice of a classification scheme for a new university or college library must always lead to much heart searching. The general schemes of classification—Dewey, UDC, Library of Congress etc—have many manifest and well publicised faults. There must always be a strong temptation to reject them in favour of a special, perhaps 'home made' scheme. However, the huge input of staff time required to devise new approaches, or radically to adapt the old, in the final analysis usually inhibits such an approach. The convenience of major bibliographies arranged by one or other of the traditional schemes, whatever their technical faults, is often overwhelmingly attractive.

Patrick Quigg's *Theory of cataloguing* (Bingley, 1968) provides a summary of current practice in relation to cataloguing in British university libraries. Quigg comments on the most important survey of practice produced by J Friedman and A Jeffreys, 'Cataloguing and classification in British university libraries: a survey of practices and procedures' *Journal of documentation* 23(3) September 1967 179-272 (and also separately published by the Sheffield University Postgraduate School of Librarianship, 1967). This survey is a most important document, providing a study of the practices of libraries based upon a detailed questionnaire. It reveals the Library of Congress classification as the most widely used, and shows that the subject catalogue is not generally favoured in British universities, the emphasis being upon 'name' catalogues. In sharp contradistinction to American practice there is no wide use made of printed catalogue cards, which can be obtained from central cataloguing agencies such as BNB or the Library of Congress.

R M Dougherty's 'The realities of re-classification' *College and research libraries* 28(4) July 1967 258-262 provides hard facts about the problems of undertaking re-classification, and leads inevitably to the conclusion that however dissatisfied one is with the classification scheme in use, there is little to be gained in most cases from a change, the effort involved hardly being balanced by any increase in efficiency to be had from a different scheme, in view of the lack of any one scheme which has really significant advantages over any other.

Just how much it costs to produce library catalogues when all the hidden costs are taken into account is revealed by R M Hayes and R M Shoffner's *The economics of book catalogue production: a study prepared for Stanford University Libraries and the Council on Library Resources* (Sherman Oaks, California, Hughes Dynamics Inc, 1964).

CHAPTER THREE
LIBRARY PLANNING, EQUIPMENT AND FITTING

THE problem for large libraries in the planning of their buildings for service is the conflict between the need to provide for large and easily extendible storage areas, and the possibility of making the service to readers as swift and efficient as possible. The larger the storage areas become, the more difficult it is to retrieve required items quickly. In view of Fremont Rider's assertion that American college and university libraries have tended to double in size every fifteen years (a claim first made in *About books* 11(1) 1940 1-11 and frequently repeated since), the problem is a very real one, despite the fact that H W Axford's 'Rider revisited' *College and research libraries* 23(4) July 345-347, in examining the validity of Rider's claims in the light of growth rates between 1946 and 1960, tends to indicate a less dramatic rate of doubling of stocks. Axford's conclusions were that the actual rate of growth over the fifteen year period he examined was some seventy eight percent overall, though with some actually exceeding the 100 percent growth rate—one of them actually achieving 190 percent growth in this period. His general conclusion was that the larger a library becomes, the slower its rate of growth—Harvard having achieved forty four percent growth in the period, Yale twenty four percent, Illinois sixty four percent and Columbia sixty eight percent. Harrison Bryan, surveying Australian university growth rates in his article 'For what they are worth' *Quill* 1(2) September 1960 20-27, revealed that Australian university libraries had an overall growth rate of about one third between the years 1950 and 1957.

What this swift growth means in terms of building university libraries is graphically portrayed in Ralph E McCoy's 'The ordeal of a university library' *Library journal* 85(9) May 1 1960 1729-1734. He describes a library which had 170,000 volumes in 1955, 350,000 in 1959 and an expected 1,000,000 volumes by 1970. McCoy chose to have his own library designed on the modular principle (a concept fully described in UNESCO *Bulletin for libraries* 17(6) November-December 1963 346-350), with the library sited right in the heart of the campus. The issue of UNESCO *Bulletin* cited above is, in fact, a special one devoted to the problems of university library buildings, and the unwillingness of librarians in Europe to adopt modular planning is severely castigated. The conservatism displayed by such librarians in continuing to plump for more ' traditional ' solutions to building problems seems illogical to the writer of the article on modular planning (W Piasecki), in view of the palpable breakdown of the effectiveness of what he terms ' the old solutions '. F G Van der Riet's ' University library planning ' *South African libraries* 27(3) January 1960 97-100 is enthusiastically modular in outlook. He provides also a thoughtful summary of the stages in the evolution of university library architecture :

1 The grand architectural manner—libraries as the vehicles for the expression of the architect's personality—an evolutionary stage displayed by buildings dating from the late nineteenth and early twentieth centuries.

2 A more realistic approach to the function of the library, as displayed in the period since the second world war, leading into the present phase:

3 The modern trend towards planned flexibility in the organization of the interior, while still maintaining a clear view of function in the planning stage.

Van der Riet also provides some useful guidance on the more mundane aspects of library planning, such as ceiling heights and flooring specifications.

The emphasis in much modern writing upon university library planning is upon the creation of interiors which will enable as much as possible of the stock to be displayed in such a way that readers can have easy and swift access to it without going through staff intermediaries. A contrary view of the problems of planning, working from a completely different starting point, is always healthy, and it is provided by K W Humphreys in his paper to the Conference of the Universities of the United Kingdom, ' University libraries ', in which he proposes a re-examination of the planning problems of university libraries. Controversially, he argues for a reversion to the closed access mode for such libraries, with the stock being compactly stored by segregation into sizes. He maintains in this very provocative article that university libraries have a tendency to store far too many books anyway, and that much marginal material should not be there at all, which would reduce the storage problems of university libraries considerably.

Undoubtedly the most important single contribution to the planning problems of university libraries in recent years has been Keyes D Metcalf's massive *Planning academic and research libraries* (McGraw Hill, 1965). This definitive text contains sections on such topics as modular construction, the problems of height, traffic flows, storage, heating, lighting and ventilation, furniture and planning.

The increasing difficulties of retrieving material from stores, which were referred to earlier, has caused great interest in the possibilities of automation of the library, not only in the context of routine clerical processes, but also in respect of physical retrieval of books from the shelves. Stanley Humenuk's ' Automatic shelving and book retrieval' (University of Illinois Graduate School of Library Science, Occasional Paper no 78) suggests that a system of keyed matrices similar to those on a linotype machine be used for the automatic shelving and retrieval of books. He argues that ' while computers are being used for various library functions, they have limited usefulness until the problem of what to do with the books is solved'. A D Osborn discusses ' The influence of automation on the design of a university library' *in* Kent *Library planning for automation* (Spartan Books, 1965) 55-73. The preliminary ideas for a library taking account of the problems of automation to the fullest extent are provided by an article in *Wilson library bulletin* 40(10) June 1966 900. This article describes the University of California (San Diego Campus) Library plans.

On the more general level of library planning, Jean Bleton in his article ' The construction of university libraries: how to plan and revise a project' UNESCO *Bulletin for libraries* 17(6) November-December 1963 309-315 draws attention so strongly to the need for the librarian to define ' from the outset clearly and precisely the function or functions the library is to fulfil vis-à-vis the users ', that one is led to suspect that he has personal experience of the difficulties of working in libraries planned without close consultation between librarian and architect. R E Ellsworth's checklist of the accommodation requirements which need to be programmed in planning a new library building, which appeared in his article

'Consultants for college and university library building planning' *College and research libraries* 21(4) July 1960 263-268, is a very valuable contribution to the literature. In the same issue of *College and research libraries*, E Green describes the 'Background activities in the planning of a new library', and indicates how a programme such as that described by Ellsworth is turned into sizes and costs through the discussions of the librarian and the architect. H L Roth's 'Planning library buildings for service' *in* the *Proceedings of a library buildings and equipment institute* July 6-8 1961 (ALA, 1964), and K A Loedwycks *Essentials of library planning* (University of Melbourne Press, 1961) are also useful reading.

On the difficult question of site selection for the university library, Keyes Metcalf comes out strongly against centre-of-campus sites in his book cited above. He believes that, given a central site, architects would find the temptation to erect an unfunctional monument quite irresistible. Less cynically but more practically, he draws attention to the fact that centrally located buildings call for access from all sides, with a consequent increase in the need for lobby and circulation space, and for an increased provision for the supervision of entrances. A central site is also likely to cause difficulties in providing for further extension of the building should that become necessary.

ALTERNATIVES TO A NEW BUILDING

It is not always possible to obtain the resources to design and build a new library in an old established university. In the case of a new foundation, the need for a library building is as manifest as the need for buildings of every other kind, but where a library building already exists it is often difficult to secure funds to provide a new one unless the old one is utterly useless. Many librarians are faced, then, with the need to adapt old buildings to fit present and future needs. Apart from the problem of providing space for additional staff, with the associated rise in the amount of space for technical processing, this implies that the other pressing problems are those already mentioned—the provision of space for storage and for more reading places for library users. These latter two problems appear, on the surface, to be in direct conflict when it is necessary to provide for them in one building of limited size. The heading of this section is the title of an article by Keyes D Metcalf in *College and research libraries* 22(5) September 1961 345-354. Metcalf makes the very valid point that a study of all of the alternatives to the provision of a new building is an essential preliminary to mounting any claim for new construction. If a claim for new construction is rejected, he says, a quick follow-up with a less expensive, but functional, alternative stands a good chance of being successful. Studies of the alternatives to new construction are specially relevant to the problems of small college libraries, confined to rooms in large blocks, rather than located on individual sites where extensions could be built on without too much disturbance.

The alternatives summarized are:

Reading areas:

a) Refurnishing will often create more reader space through the use of better designed and more functional furnishing—many older library buildings feature heavy, ornate furniture, which is difficult to move about and very space consuming.

b) Older library buildings often feature hallways, lobbies and wide corridors, which represent an inefficient use of space. They can be fitted out as exhibition spaces and thus release rooms previously used for such purposes for reader services. Large entrance halls can be adapted to become catalogue halls and enquiry and service counter areas, with a consequent release of space for reading tables in the library proper. Non-public corridors can be lined with shelving to provide extra storage space.

c) Large, high ceilinged reading rooms were often a feature of old library buildings. They can be successfully adapted by the addition of mezzanine floors or galleries to accommodate more readers and more book shelving.

d) In small colleges, where the library is located in one or more rooms within a larger building, it is often possible to exchange the library room for a larger one—for example, by swapping the functions of a lecture theatre or a machine room.

e) Departmental collections might be established in other buildings in an effort to reduce pressure on the main library.

Storage areas:

a) The existing stores may be reshelved with compact shelving on rollers. Stock might be ' double banked ' on existing shelves, or reorganized into several parallel sequences, according to size, to make the greatest use of the available shelf space.

b) Older and less used stock may be moved to stores away from the campus, where rental or building costs are lower.

c) A programme of micro-recording older stock and runs of periodicals may be adopted.

d) Little used stock may well be disposed of, and greater reliance placed upon co-operative schemes.

Staff and technical services space:

The redesign of these areas is likely to cause most difficulty, since these are the areas which are traditionally the meanest in initial provision. The following are some of the measures which might be taken to improve arrangements:

1 The relocation of much of the technical services work—perhaps by securing rented premises elsewhere.

2 Introducing more mechanization or automation of technical services work might result in the improvement of productivity within the same basic area.

3 Often one of the greatest problems is the provision of additional offices for senior members of staff. This can sometimes be achieved by the subdivision of one or two large rooms into a series of small offices.

4 When space is very limited and none of the above methods results in any great improvement in efficiency over a long period, then it is essential that a firm of management consultants should be called in to advise on the replanning of space to improve overall efficiency of use of the available rooms.

NEW BUILDINGS

When a feasibility study of the means of adapting old premises to new uses has been done, the result may be that the authorities become convinced that a new building would be at least as economic in the long run, and it is therefore useful to consider some of the points which should be borne in mind in planning new buildings.

The most basic point is that the recent history of the growth of academic and national libraries should be regarded in making any plans. There is no reason to believe that the rate of expansion of such libraries will fall in the future. It is therefore essential to plan buildings for maximum flexibility. Interior layouts must be capable of easy and cheap replanning. The sites upon which buildings are put must provide enough space for the possibilities of a great deal of expansion work to be carried out.

The greatest need in academic and national libraries is for a lavish provision of storage areas, though it should be remembered that since storage areas can only be thought of as economic when they are in full use, it is probably better not to provide, initially, storage areas which will remain empty for many years, but to make site provision which will enable further increments of space to be added to the storage areas without too much difficulty at a later stage.

SOME SPECIAL POINTS CONCERNING NATIONAL LIBRARIES

If a national library is near to or within a very large centre of population, then a large provision of reading accommodation will need to be made. When the national library is located in a smaller centre of population—Canberra or Aberystwyth are examples—then the provision of reading areas will not need to be so great.

While siting is best effected near to a large centre of population, it must not be forgotten that this can limit physical growth if the library becomes 'boxed in' by other development—the recent difficulties of the British Museum Library is one example, in sharp distinction to the availability of (at present) almost limitless growth potential for the National Lending Library for Science and Technology at rural Boston Spa. An interesting note on the requirements to be met in planning national library buildings is given in UNESCO *Bulletin for libraries* 18(4) July-August 1964 157. It should not be forgotten that the accommodation requirements of a national library will often need to include provision for a national bibliographical centre and also, perhaps, a library school.

THE SCALE OF THE ACCOMMODATION PROVISION

This depends upon many factors. Is it, for example, the policy of the library to restrict borrowing rights? If so, then there is a need to provide rather more in the way of reading spaces than would otherwise be the case. Another factor for academic libraries to consider in relation to planning is the pattern of teaching. If teaching is largely based upon formal lectures, with little requirement of students to do extra reading on their own, then the library seating accommodation may be much less lavish in its provision, than in an organization where there is a high degree of 'self organization' of study, through tutorial and seminar methods based upon the submission of essays and projects. In terms of library seating accommodation, the difference in the needs of the two systems might be seats for ten percent of the student population under the former and forty percent under the latter. The AUT survey recommends that thirty three percent of the student population of a college or university should be able to find seats in the library at any one time.

OTHER POINTS TO NOTE

There is a strong demand in academic libraries for the provision of study areas, not necessarily with a full library service available, which are open until late in the day. The need is, quite simply, for working space adequately lit and heated and with a reasonable degree of quietness, not least in view of the frequently poor living conditions in which students exist while at university. There is also a need for rooms in which smoking is permitted and for others in which typewriters and business machines can be used. When the university or college campus is far from the halls of residence, there will be a demand for car parking facilities, and possibly, in those circumstances, even a snack-bar.

CHAPTER FOUR: STAFF

THE lack of any significant literature from British sources on the problems of staffing academic libraries seems to point to a possible undervaluation of human resources in such libraries. The staffing budget is, in fact, inevitably the largest single item in the estimates of expenditure. The available literature largely seeks to explain the functions and responsibilities of the various grades of staff, without any analysis of the problems involved.

To secure an adequate appreciation of the nature of the human relations and management problems to be met with in staffing libraries, the librarian must be prepared to read broadly in the literature of industrial personnel management, looking at problems of welfare, communications and management development, and he must seek to relate findings in the larger world to the field of librarianship. There are a large number of valuable management texts and it would be difficult to give a short list which can satisfy everybody. The following are books which may be read with profit, though these are not the only, or necessarily the most comprehensive, texts of a general nature for the librarian to read:
R F Tredgold *Human relations in modern industry* (Duckworth),
T M Ling *Mental health and human relations in industry* (H K Lewis),
W V Merrihue *Managing by communications* (McGraw-Hill), and
P Garforth *Management development* (Institute of Personnel Management).

Librarians need to overcome any aversion they might feel to the study of personnel management, and realize that librarianship does not exist as a separate world to which the problems in other spheres of activity can have no relevance. It is proposed here to present a list of the areas in which problems appear to exist in the staffing of national and academic libraries, and then to provide some elaboration of them.

STAFFING PROBLEMS
1 The difficulties caused by the divisions into various grades,

depending upon educational level reached by staff. Training and development needs.

2 Subject specialization of staff tends to create 'backwaters' which do not provide the best training for promotion in general administration. The lack of scientifically qualified staff.

3 Academic status and salary levels. Are they realistically equated with other areas?

4 The closed nature of many national libraries, which provide 'cradle to grave' careers.

1 *The interaction of the grades of staff/training needs*: The multiplicity of grades of staff in the typical university or national library is a barrier to the creation of corporate spirit. In any one library there may be staff in each of the following grades—graduate librarians, non-graduate professional librarians, non-graduate library assistants (without professional qualifications), clerical staff (secretaries, typists, machine operators etc), skilled manual workers, unskilled manual workers (porters, cleaners etc). There are even sophisticated variations within grades; for example a distinction is often made between 'good' honours degrees, honours degrees, and 'ordinary' (pass) graduates, as well as between arts and science graduates. To observe what will happen to the CNAA graduate in this atmosphere is likely to provide much interest in the next few years.

With so many distinctive grades, a community of interest is not easy to create. The staff in the various grades tend to form 'status groups' within each, and to take up defensive attitudes towards each other. Demarcation disputes, so much reviled in industry, are not unknown in academic libraries. Non-graduate staff with professional qualifications can be quite as effective in certain roles as graduate staff, but may find themselves baulked in the promotion ladder at low salaries, above which they can rise only with extreme difficulty. Non-graduate professional personnel often complain of subordination to graduate librarians unwilling, and sometimes utterly unable, to see their administrative points of view. Fortunately, there is a growing tendency for some academic libraries to reduce the amount of structuring in their gradings, and to recognize the value of promoting, at least in the lower senior ranks, purely on merit in the job, rather than primarily upon pre-entry qualification levels.

As far as training provision goes, British national and university libraries do not have a good record in providing facilities for staff to qualify for promotion. There has been no very explicit policy, for example, in allowing non-graduate staff special facilities for reading for degrees, or for junior graduate staff to research for higher degrees. The essential corollary to any complex structure of gradings must surely be the availability of facilities for staff to equip themselves to progress through them. The Standing Conference of National and University Libraries (SCONUL) is currently greatly interested in the problem of staff training, as D T Richnell indicates in ' Education for librarians and information officers' *Journal of documentation* 22(4) December 1966 291-300. Comparative material indicating that the problems of the division of staff by grades of qualification and type of work are not simply British are provided by the following references to American literature: R H Muller ' Principles governing the employment of non-professional personnel in university libraries' *College and research libraries* 26(3) May 1965 225-227. D C Weber ' The place of " professional specialists " in the university library staff' *College and research libraries* 26(5) September 1965 383-388. E Kanasy ' Division of labour in technical service departments' *Ontario library review* 47(3) August 1963 91-92. W H Jesse ' Inter-personnel relations in libraries' *College and research libraries* 21(2) March 1960 149-155. Suggested standards for the provision of staff for university libraries are given in The Association of University Teacher's policy document *The university library* (1964), and the same body's *British universities annual 1965* contains a most useful article by Maurice Line on ' Staffing university libraries ', pp 93-99.

2 *Subject specialization*: Most national and university libraries practice some degree of specialization by subject, or by literary form. The problem for them is the lack of enough librarians with specialist qualifications in, for example, science, orientalia, or in the librarianship areas of maps, manuscripts or rare books. Specialists run the considerable risk of becoming cut off in their specialization, left aside from the main promotion streams because their, usually, small departments do not give them the opportunity to demonstrate the administrative skills considered indivisible from promotion to higher grades. Their main compensations are the bargaining power of scarcity, and their opportunities for great satisfaction in their work, which lie in their close relationships

with their specialist users, in a manner not open to colleagues in the more general areas of librarianship. Two articles on the role of subject specialists are K Humphreys ' The subject specialist in national and university libraries ' *Libri* 17(1) 1965 29-41, and J P Danton ' The subject specialist in national and university libraries, with special reference to book selection ' *Libri* 17(1) 1967 42-58.

3 *Status and salaries*: The equation of the salaries of the higher grades of national and university library staffs with those enjoyed by higher grade civil servants or higher grade academic teaching staff is by no means a common occurrence in many countries. The difficulties seem to centre around a tendency to integrate librarians' salaries at a point in an overall grading structure which produces equation of senior grade library personnel with teaching personnel of much lower responsibility levels and educational pre-entry requirements. Instances of the existence of such problems can be seen reported in *Library trends* 4(1) 1955 81-88. Insofar as national and university libraries are concerned in the United Kingdom, this is not a very great problem. University librarians are recognized as being full professors for salary purposes, and their subordinate graduate and senior professional personnel are usually satisfactorily integrated into the academic staff grades for salary purposes. In the British national libraries, civil service pay and conditions apply in such a way that senior staff are paid on scales equivalent to quite senior civil servants, and their junior staffs on the appropriate scales for such staffs in the civil service generally. It is in the further education colleges and college of education that much work still remains to be done in the creation of staffing structures which provide career facilities for library staff as attractive as those for teaching staff. Not all librarians in colleges of these kinds are yet regarded as senior members of the academic staff; some are, regrettably, still considered as adjuncts of the clerical and administrative staff.

The American literature on the subject of academic library staffing indicates that there is much insecurity and dissatisfaction with the lack of proper integration with teaching staff in many academic libraries in the USA. There appears to be an almost pathological preoccupation with status problems. As indicated above, while there is some difficulty in lesser colleges in the United Kingdom, high academic status and membership of the appropriate governing and administrative organs is the rule rather than the exception in Britain. W L Guttsman's 'Learned librarians and the structure of academic libraries' *Libri* 15(2) 1965 159-167 is an important statement of the British point of view, while R B Downs examines the practice of American universities in 'The status of American college and university librarians' ACRL *Monographs* (22) 1958. This latter study is up-dated to a certain extent by V R Neghorbon's 'Faculty rank and faculty status amongst librarians' *Catholic library world* 35 May 1964 551-553. That the preoccupation with improving the status of academic librarians is not purely an American phenomenon is indicated by an anonymous article in UNESCO *Bulletin for libraries* 17(3) May-June 1963 169-174 entitled 'A profile of the university libraries in one country'.

4 *The closed nature of national library appointments*: The *Library trends* issue cited above deals extensively with national library staffing, and indicates that the recruitment and retention of adequate staff is almost always a problem. In the United Kingdom the position is reasonable, with an adequate, if not specially exciting career prospect available. The pension arrangements and the nature of the work undertaken in the national libraries does tend to oblige staff to stay within the one institution all their lives, however. Such a situation has both good and bad effects. It is good that continuity of experience is available in such institutions, and good also that salaries are reasonable enough to persuade people of good calibre to stay. It is bad, however, that there is a lack of cross-fertilization of ideas between the national and other types of libraries in the country, with the consequent possibility of greater inventiveness in solving problems in both spheres thus effectively sealed off. In the United States there is a tradition of exchange of jobs between the Library of Congress and other, usually university, libraries. Exchanges have often been highly successful, suggesting that there are, indeed, benefits to be derived from the practice. It is, perhaps, the fact that there are virtually no other libraries in Britain of a scale even remotely comparable to that of the British Museum that has inhibited inter-changes here. The difference in scale between the British Museum's six to seven million volumes, and the average of less than half a million volumes in university libraries, is probably greater than that between the Library of Congress collection and the several million volumes held by the top ten or so American universities.

CHAPTER FIVE: STOCK

THE late Lord Leverhulme used to say that he reckoned half of the money spent by his companies on advertising was wasted, but the trouble was that he did not know which half! Modern research libraries, faced with an increasing flow of new publications from which to select the additions to their already overcrowded stores, know the feeling. A proportion of their current selections, like their past selections, will be little used or even totally unused. A significant proportion of the effort put into the acquisition of books from all over the world comes to nothing, simply because some items selected remain unused. Obviously, if the proportion of books unused is large, then the acquisition policy of the particular library is at fault, but it must be accepted that, no matter how careful the library, a small proportion of the current acquisitions will be little used. Could scientific methods be employed to assist in book selection? Are there statistical techniques which could be employed to decide in advance which material will have a lasting significance? Probably this will never be wholly possible, but there are some sophisticated techniques available to assist in the recognition of materials in store which may safely be weeded out. A most interesting project, which aims at eliminating some of the chance elements in the withdrawal of books from store, is described by Lee Ash in *Yale's selective book retirement program* (Hamden, Conn, Archon Books, 1963).

Librarians who collect widely and undogmatically may do so out of fear that to do otherwise would result in a repetition of Bodley's famous blunders, when he laid down the policy to be followed by his librarian in book selection. They are also in a position to be aware of the deficiencies of their stocks as a result of the failings of their predecessors. Librarians are also apt to place exaggerated faith in the partial solutions to their worst book selection problems which have been devised—inter-library co-operation, subject specialization, storage libraries and microrecording.

The *Parry report*, p 62, makes the point that every academic library should have an explicit acquisitions policy. J Orne's 'Current trends in collection development in university libraries' *Library trends* 15(2) October 1966 provides some indications of the points which need to be borne in mind in drawing up a policy of selection. Other useful articles dealing with the general problem are R Haro 'Book selection in academic libraries' *College and research libraries* 28(2) March 1967 104-106, and P M Benjamin 'Feed and weed: a philosophy of book selection' *College and research libraries* 23(6) November 1962 500-503.

The central problem of book selection for the research library is exposed by J H P Pafford in his important article 'Book selection in the university library' UNESCO *Bulletin for libraries* 17(1) January-February 1963 12-16. Major reference works and important evaluatively-reviewed books by acknowledged authorities, and well tried undergraduate texts, says Pafford, virtually select themselves. It is the large mass of secondary material and items from new and unknown sources which pose the problem. This is where some of the next generation's gold lies inextricably mixed with much of its dross. Pafford also draws attention to the relationship between acquisition and withdrawal policy. Most of the scientifically planned investigations into selection problems concern periodicals. E P Tober's 'Determining optimal back number inventories' *American documentation* 10(3) July 1959 224-227 indicates the problem and poses tentative solutions.

NATIONAL LIBRARIES AND STOCK SELECTION

An increasing proportion of the accessions of national libraries arise out of exchange agreements. UNESCO has been active in promoting the development of international exchange agreements. The *Handbook on the international exchange of publications* is supported by regular notes in UNESCO *Bulletin for libraries*. Obviously, where a library has significant amounts of material which it is able to exchange, say second copies of material legally deposited, and can obtain useful material in exchange, much benefit accrues to all parties (except the publishers!). This is especially so when finances are either limited or unconvertible because of national or international policy. A warning must be sounded, however, since the large amount of staff time involved in the administration of exchange schemes is often disproportionate to the benefits gained. If this is the only method whereby important materials can be obtained, however, then it is a method which must be adopted.

Legal deposit is, of course, a most important source of acquisition in national libraries, though some national libraries do not enjoy the privilege. Deposit does have associated problems. The large bulk of the material received causes storage difficulties, and often there is no means of effecting withdrawal of this material, due to the governing regulations which insist that all material taken must be permanently stored. Because deposited items must be carefully preserved, it is often necessary to buy duplicate copies of books in transient demand to ensure this preservation. The advent of extensive co-operative acquisition programmes by groups of libraries other than the national library has caused a decline in the importance of preservation for posterity as an aim of legal deposit in national libraries. Of greater significance in the policy of national libraries in book selection now is the acquisition of foreign material.

The sources from which significant materials can be acquired by libraries have multiplied and diversified considerably in the last few years. Studies by the Farmington Plan Administration (see chapter eight) have revealed that there are often unexpectedly rich sources of recorded knowledge in areas such as the Middle East and South East Asia. In many countries, only the national library and, perhaps, the major academic libraries can be expected to be well organized enough to acquire large quantities of foreign material systematically. Other libraries often lack the essential bibliographical records, or they do not have staffs either large enough or skilled enough to deal with a multiplicity of suppliers in many countries.

ACADEMIC LIBRARIES

A major book selection problem for academic libraries is to strike a proper balance between undergraduate and research needs. Another problem is that of balancing the available purchase funds between departments. This is not a simple matter of arithmetic, for the needs of different subjects must be assessed in bibliographic terms, and given a ' weighting ' according to an estimate of the value of library materials in that subject field as compared to, say, laboratory equipment in the teaching of the subject. Some disciplines rely more heavily than others upon expensive primary source materials. While science and technology is often thought of as having strong claims on the available funds in view of the 'literature explosion' in that field, it ought to be remembered that basic scientific teaching equipment—microscopes, computers etc, are financed out of special funds and are not a call upon the library. Basic equipment for the English department may, on the other hand, comprise a collection of autograph letters, for example, yet these may fall as a charge on library funds. Library requirements of non-science/technology departments cannot, therefore, be allowed to become submerged under the raucous publicity associated with the contemporary need to collect vast quantities of technical literature.

The allocation of funds for book purchase between subjects must take account, also, of the teaching practices and methods in different departments. Programmes which are primarily lecture-based often require students to have ready access to a small number of basic texts. When courses are based largely upon the tutorial assessment of individually assigned work, there is a corresponding need for students to have access to a wide range of material, rather than to have heavy emphasis placed upon one or two textbooks. The amount of research already being carried out, or the possibility of the development of research efforts within particular departments also needs to be taken into account when deciding upon the allocation of funds.

Effective deployment of funds depends upon the number of separate service points which a library has. When there are several service points, overheads will be greater proportionately, because of the necessity to duplicate basic reference books, such as dictionaries, encyclopedias and bibliographies at the various service points. Another consideration to be weighed in deciding upon the allocation of financial resources is the assessment of the prospects of co-operation with local public and special libraries in the provision of certain specialized resources. Too often this is not given the consideration it deserves, for co-operation can be of particular benefit in the rationalization of periodical holdings, both in respect of back files and of current accessions. But co-operation works both ways, and this, of itself, may add further difficulties and expense.

INTERNAL ORGANIZATION OF BOOK SELECTION

The practice of book selection in academic libraries is widely varied. In some institutions the major responsibility for the initiation of suggestions for purchase comes from the teaching staff, with the librarian playing only a limited role. In other instances the librarian plays the major role, though obviously he pays due attention to the suggestions of the academic staff. In many European countries, the book selection for the university library is entirely in the hands of the library staff, whereas, in most British and American institutions, measures are devised to ensure that there is some degree of joint consultation. Teaching staff in this latter situation are often looked to as the final arbiters of quality in respect of material to be added to stock, but the librarian considers carefully the overall balance of stock, and is likely to reserve to himself the tasks of rectifying any imbalance which he discerns, and of providing the supporting reference books and bibliographies.

In those European countries in which the library staff do all the selection, it lies in the hands of librarians who are also subject specialists. This is probably the ideal solution to the problem of book selection, but it does require the librarian/specialist concerned to be in constant and close touch with the teaching—and this is not often the case in the universities of Western Europe. Wilson and Tauber note in *The university library* (Columbia University Press, 1956) that the librarian/subject specialist approach is the one in use at the New York Public Library, and it is their claim that this approach produces a selection process which results in the purchase of a greater number of titles which later emerge as standard works than does any other method of selection. Teaching staff naturally suggest materials for selection which meet their own immediate needs, rather than further the ultimate benefit of the library viewed as a permanent and dynamic entity. They can in this matter hardly be expected to take account of the broader philosophies which impel a librarian. It is for this reason, as much as any other, that the librarian must be a leader in the selection process, providing the guidance for the final balance struck.

SPECIAL COLLECTIONS

These are obtained, in nucleus or in toto, either by donation or purchase. Donations of notable collections tend to be attracted by those libraries which already have an established reputation, though it would be morally wrong for such a library to accept a donation unless it added significantly to the existing academic purposes of the institution. Too often, collections are donated and accepted simply as embellishments to a stock rather than as contributions to the library's central purpose.

There are other circumstances, however, which affect the decision to accept an offered collection. Will it, for example, require any special storage arrangements and, if so, can these be provided without detriment to the existing pattern of service? Another question which should always be asked is 'Are there any limiting conditions upon use or disposal of the donation?'. Too often in the past, large collections of much worthless material have been accepted by libraries with conditions attached which call, for example, for the material to be kept together inviolate, when, in fact, the library has accepted the collection simply because there are a small number of items in the collection which are of value. If it is a condition of the sale or donation of a collection, that it be kept together inviolate and for all time, then the librarian may face unpleasant decisions. Unless his need for the few required items within the collection is specially great, he is probably wise to refuse its acquisition.

STANDARDS OF STOCK

There are many *dicta* purporting to recommend minimum sizes of stock, 'ideal' bookfunds, minimum standards for levels of expenditure and so on. They all need to be approached with caution, for they can usually take no account of the existing size and quality of a bookstock, or of the differing levels of demand made on bookstocks, in different establishments. Standards which specify an expenditure of so many pounds or shillings per head of the student body are unhelpful, in the absence of an assessment of the levels of need of students in different teaching situations, and at different educational levels. Such a standard does not usually take account of the fact that institutions with small student bodies may still need a stock which is as diversified as that of a larger institution able to enjoy some economy of scale. R W Trueswell's 'Determining the optimal number of volumes for a library's core collection' *Libri* 16(1) 49-60 provides some interesting statistical backing for this last statement.

Standards which provide a basis for the continuation at a reasonable level of a well established and efficiently run library can nevertheless prove totally inadequate for a new library, or one badly run down and in need of special treatment. The proposition of basic standards can be a two-edged weapon. Levels which prove a goad to the backward might, at the same time, represent an embarrassment to the progressive.

While not mentioning standards recommendations specifically, James Thompson's ' University libraries and higher education ' *Library Association record* 66(11) November 1964 466-471 points out the unreality of thinking in terms of the proposition of minima in a country such as the United Kingdom, where basic adequacy is the mark of the better libraries. He feels that the only comparisons which have any meaning are those with situations in other countries. Although it is easy to shrug off the unhappy comparisons which can be made with some libraries in the United States, on the grounds of the greater economic strength of that country as compared to the United Kingdom, it is less easy to explain away similar comparisons with libraries in Europe. It is less easy still to justify the greater speed of growth to front rank of some university libraries in the Commonwealth countries.

It is necessary here to point out that there are a number of minimum standards statements available for different types of academic library, notably those issued by the Library Association for colleges of education and for technical colleges, and those of the Association of University Teachers for university libraries; but it is not unfair to claim that in individual situations they have often proved so inadequate in practice as to be a positive barrier to progress. A further stratum to the business of proposing standards of service is provided by the Library Association's ' Libraries in the new polytechnics ' *Library Association record* 70(9) September 1968 240-243. As an illustration of the hazards facing the proposers of standards, this latter case is instructive, since the burden of criticism so far apparent is that these standards are so much ahead of existing levels of provision in the colleges emerging to polytechnic status as to be unreal.

There is not, and probably never can be, an adequate basis for the proposition of minimum stock standards. The only standard a library can operate is the competent deployment of the largest amount of money for purchase which an imaginative librarian can obtain, in order to fulfil clearly articulated objectives which have been drawn up in consultation with library users. It is a great source of fascination (and frustration) that stock building objectives change as a library grows. A plan which was intended to raise the quality of a stock to a level at which it could fulfil all the foreseeable demands likely to be made of it, rarely succeeds, simply because the attainment of objectives inevitably reveals further objectives which in their turn must be reached.

CHAPTER SIX: SPECIAL DEPARTMENTS AND COLLECTIONS

MERGERS, takeovers and amalgamations in industry and commerce occur, amongst other things, to reap the benefit of economies of scale in production. By introducing specialized handling, production and accounting methods, and creating more highly specialized staffing units, a higher rate of output may be obtained from the two merged units than previously was the case from the two separated units.

In terms of the library, this situation is less clear-cut. Large units, such as university or national libraries, can, it is true, reap great benefits of staffing economy by the centralization of routine processes. The larger the library becomes, however, the greater the need for the creation of a structure of subject and functional departments, to increase the standard of service to readers and ensure the full utilization of stock. Large general libraries, without some departmental division, become very cumbersome to use, because their size makes the speedy retrieval of desired items from storage areas very difficult. Staff handling such large general collections are unlikely to be able to bring the same degree of administrative and professional skill to the task of reader service in this environment, as would be possible if they were given some specialization of subject or literary form to work in. The usual solution adopted is to divide a large library into a series of departments or sections according to one of several basic philosophies. The price of sub-division into smaller units is that, inevitably, more staff are needed to provide the more intensive service to be expected from the smaller units. Administrative overheads are also greater, and the amount of accommodation required by a collection of subject departments is usually more extensive than that required by one integrated unit.

The larger inputs of staff arise principally out of the need to provide at least minimum staff cover of the public service at all times when the library is open. The more intensive service likely to result from subject division is brought about by the fact that the division of the library stock into smaller and more specialized elements brings into sharper focus the potentialities of the stock, to both staff and library users. The staff obtain a clearer idea of the desirable goals of their provision, and the library users make more insistent demands upon a service which they can clearly see to be of a specialized nature. It is an interesting fact that the good specialized library often seems to attract a greater amount of criticism than the poor general library, simply because people come to expect more of it.

NATIONAL LIBRARIES

These tend to be divided up according to the physical form of the material—printed books, manuscripts, maps, music etc. This makes a subject approach to the use of such libraries difficult. This is, perhaps, not too serious a problem where the national library is regarded as simply a library of last recourse for individual items of material unobtainable in other, lesser, libraries. Where the national library is itself intending to be a front rank general research library for work of long duration and deep specialization, however, as indeed most national libraries try to be, the lack of a subject organization of the stock is a major source of difficulty for users and staff alike. Another difficulty in many national libraries is the existence of special collections which cut across the basic pattern of organization, and which are kept in remote parts of the library and are often inaccessible to readers. The approach to the organization of the library materials by physical form produces situations in which the reader finds it difficult to gather together collections of material to work on. He is often obliged to move from place to place, consulting state papers in one part of the library, moving to the manuscript department for other items, while, at the same time, trying to carry out the bulk of his work from a base in the department of printed books.

 The symposium on national libraries in Europe in 1958 came out strongly in favour of a measure of decentralization for national library stock, though it rejected the possibility of breaking up the national library into a series of special subject libraries. Division of the stock by subject within the framework of a single library organization was, however, thought to be essential, to ensure that the most effective use be made of the rapidly increasing stocks of such libraries. This was thought to be especially the case in the exploitation of the scientific and technical stock. L Quincy Mumford has discussed the role of the national library in the provision of scientific and technical information in some detail, in a paper to the Asian Regional Seminar on National Libraries organized by UNESCO; the paper was reprinted in UNESCO *Bulletin for libraries* 18(4) July-August 1964 172-177, 192.

ACADEMIC LIBRARIES
Whether the desires of individual departments and teaching divisions within universities and colleges for their own separate library provision adjacent to their teaching areas should be acceded to is, perhaps, the greatest single organizational problem in the academic library field. P Havard Williams, in an article ' The modern university library ' UNESCO *Bulletin for libraries* 13(5-6) May-June 1959 110-114, felt that the demands of departments for their own libraries were a criticism of the main library. This may, indeed, be so, but there are probably other issues which cause such demands to be made, notably the great area of the modern university campus, which renders use of the main university library comparatively difficult.

The problem of the departmentalization of university libraries has been much written about in the past few years. R S Smith ' The special library in the university ' in *The two cultures, the proceedings of the Reference, Special and Information Section of the Library Association 1961* (Library Association, 1962) describes the pattern of organization of the Science Library at the University of Nottingham, and makes a strong point of the need to create a staffing structure flexible enough to make full use of the talents of both librarians and subject specialists. The question of how to break down a large library into units of a size comprehensible to and convenient for users, has three principal aspects. Firstly, it is possible to break the library down into subject divisions under the control of their own subject specialists/librarians, while still retaining them, physically, within one building. Secondly, they may be spread throughout the campus under the control of the university librarian, but carry out their functions in close association with specific departments of the university teaching. They may, in extreme cases, be outside the control of the university librarian, as has already been mentioned. The third aspect is that in which the university library is totally unsubdivided, with little regard being paid to the convenience of the teaching needs of the university, other than the availability of the library to any who will journey to it. In a regrettably inaccessible source, Archie L McNeal discusses ' Divisional organization in the university library' *University of Tennessee Library Lecture 1961* (covered by *Library science abstracts* 11416). This piece examines the advantages and disadvantages of such a system, as seen through the practices of thirteen American university libraries. ' Centralization and decentralization in academic libraries: a symposium ' *College and research libraries* 22(5) September 1961 327-337, and Neal Harlow's 'An open skies system of academic library services ' *Journal of education for librarianship* 2(4) Spring 1962 183-190, both discuss aspects of the problem. Harlow makes mention of his approval of the idea of subject divisional libraries, but deplores the general tendency towards the creation of special collections, which are often unrelated to the teaching needs of the university, and which are more usually standing collections of ' books beautiful ' or memorials to long dead scholars.

AN APPRAISAL OF THE SEVERAL METHODS OF ORGANIZING DIVISIONAL LIBRARIES

Independent departmental entities: This method is the one extensively practised on the continent of Europe, where such libraries are commonly called ' institute ' libraries. Robert Vosper's ' European university libraries . . .' issue of *Library trends* 12(4) April 1964 can be seen constantly returning to the theme of the difficulties caused by such a pattern of organization, whether it be in the section dealing with the practice of Spanish, Italian, German or, indeed, in any other of the many countries covered in this most informative volume. It is shown to be uneconomic on grounds of staffing, acquisition policy or use of space. There is a great deal of duplication of effort and of library materials, and users of such collections tend to be ignorant of the value of adequate general bibliographical support to their subject fields, and unaware of the possible use of source materials in subject areas peripheral to their own. H Tveteras, in his thoughtful article ' The university library and the institute libraries . . .' *Libri* 9(1) 1959 1-8, describes the methods used in Norway to overcome the principal difficulties encountered in attempting to bring the institute libraries into the sphere of influence of the main university library. Rightly, he stresses that the main university library staff need to take up positive attitudes to the provision of service to departments. (A real problem in many European countries is the curious lack of recognition of the university library as a central teaching organ in the university on the part of the university library staff.) By stressing their ability to give good service to departments, Tveteras feels that university library staffs will be able to prove beyond doubt their professional competence and, indeed, their academic distinction, and, in so doing, gain the confidence of the staffs and students of teaching departments, who have often received miserable library service from their own jealously guarded independent libraries.

Departments under main library control: This method of organization is the compromise often practised in universities between a system of independent departmental libraries and complete centralization in one library. It allows some central control of acquisitions to be practised, and thus ensures that expensive general reference works such as bibliographies are not extensively duplicated, or that too many copies of individual periodical titles are not bought. The main library control of staffing ensures that both standards of staffing and levels of staffing are uniform throughout the university. With central staff control it is also possible to ensure that there is a certain amount of staff inter-change, especially at the junior levels, to maintain a broadly based training for all staff. Specialist services of main library staffs in the fields of cataloguing and general administration can be harnessed to enable staffs at the departmental level to spend the greater proportion of their time in direct contact with readers.

There are circumstances wherein too much centralization of administration and staffing is not possible, due to the specialist nature of the librarianship being undertaken. Such is the case, for example, in music, maps and manuscript libraries. The work in these sections is often such that only specialists working with their own funds and administrative and cataloguing arrangements can cope with the problems.

It must be appreciated that there are circumstances within specific universities which may dictate that the various alternative methods of organization will exist side by side in the same institution—the incredibly complex networks of London and Harvard universities are cases in point, as indeed are the college/department/main library structures of Oxford and Cambridge universities. D W Butcher illustrates the range of departmental library activity in one university in his 'The departmental libraries of Cambridge University' *Journal of documentation* 7(4) December 1951 221-243. The powerful service which a well organized departmental library can give is nowhere more clearly demonstrated than in L Partington's 'The library of the Economic Growth Centre at Yale University' *Library Association record* 68(1) January 1966 13-15. This article draws attention to the increasing tendency for teaching specialists in universities to demand 'special library' standards of library service, with intensely personal service to readers, combined with the production of current-awareness bulletins, and all the other devices of the well organized special library. David W Heron's 'The centrifugence of university libraries' *College and research libraries* 23(3) May 1962 223-226 is an article which deserves close attention, since it is probably the best single modern piece analysing the problem of departmental and divisional libraries in a university.

The undergraduate collection: Whether or not there should be a special library provision specifically geared to the curricular needs of undergraduates is another of the major unresolved issues in university library administration. L Hurt *The university library and undergraduate instruction: an analysis of their relationship* (University of California Press, 1936), which is now available in a reprint from University Microfilms, is the first important contribution to this problem, and it has been well supported by further writing since.

Advocates of separate provision maintain that the size of the main library tends to overwhelm the undergraduate students and that the relative difficulty in finding materials appropriate to their level of need can provoke 'anti-library' feelings in undergraduates. It is argued that to provide a separate library with a special staff not only takes the strain off the resources of the main library, but also improves the possibilities of making undergraduates library conscious, through providing them with a service fitted to their needs.

Opponents of the special undergraduate library provision argue that to pre-digest library material at a relatively low level does nothing to demonstrate to undergraduates in their most formative years the power of a large library collection, or give them the incentive to delve deeply and range widely in their readings in a chosen subject field.

B S Page, in his paper 'University library development' *Library Association, Proceedings of the Annual Conference 1957* 52-57, refers to the need to provide a reference service to students administered by what he calls a 'student consultant'. His further point that there is a need to encourage undergraduates to read widely for recreation, as well as for instruction, is one which some universities are aware of. W B Kuhn's article 'Princeton's new Julian Street Library' *College and research libraries* 23(6) November 1962 504-508 describes how this combination of instruction and recreation is accomplished at one university. The 'house libraries' at Harvard and, to a lesser extent, the college libraries at Oxford and Cambridge universities also illustrate this principle in operation.

One factor arguing in favour of a separate provision at the undergraduate level is that it enables more effective control of multiple copies of textbooks to be maintained. T H Bowyer in his article 'Considerations on book provision for undergraduates in British university libraries' *Journal of documentation* 19(4) December 1963 151-167, and the Association of University Teachers survey *The university library* (AUT, 1964) both make the point that undergraduates do not, themselves, buy enough books to cover their basic needs. Even if they can be encouraged, or in some way obliged, to buy their own seminal texts, the problem still remains of those books which, though vitally needed for a short time during the study of relatively minor aspects of the course, are not sufficiently important to warrant a student purchasing them. It is here that the university library undergraduate collection can help by the provision of multiple copies. A contribution towards the solution of the problem is made in some American university bookshops and private organizations by the provision of rental copies of texts. Some universities recognize the value of a rental service by providing it with a subsidy. While rental collections are independent of the university library, they obviously help considerably in the solution of one of the most pressing problems facing the libraries.

It hardly needs to be stated that where an undergraduate collection exists, no barriers must be placed in the way of students who wish to make use of the main university library. A summary of the case for the provision of a separate undergraduate collection is made by F H Wagman ' Library service to undergraduate college students ' *College and research libraries* 17(2) March-April 1956 143-148.

Paragraphs 137 and 138 of the *Parry report* refer to the problem of undergraduate collections in most interesting terms: (Para 137) ' In the United States, one important result of the establishment of undergraduate libraries has been the increasing use made by undergraduates of the graduate library. It may well be that the habit of personal search inculcated within the manageable limits of an undergraduate collection has encouraged students to make use of the more complicated catalogues and much bigger collections.' (Para 138) ' It was pointed out by several librarians in America that the term " undergraduate library " no longer adequately described the institution. They were becoming collections of heavily used material frequently resorted to by graduates and even members of staff as well as undergraduates.'

Undergraduate collections, browsing rooms and halls of residence libraries are dealt with at some length in the *Parry report* pages 44-49.

Wilson library bulletin 36(10) June 1962 788 provides a news note on a most interesting example of a situation such as that mentioned in the *Parry report*, wherein the undergraduate collection serves wider needs: ' The University of Washington Library has begun an undergraduate book collection which will eventually consist of about 100,000 items, with as many copies of each title as may be necessary to meet demands . . . The collection will duplicate titles found in other parts of the library system and will contain as many copies of each title as demand will warrant. This library for undergraduates, broad in its coverage and amply equipped with books, should help relieve faculty members from dependence upon textbooks in many areas of instruction.'

SPECIAL COLLECTIONS

Consider the several forms—collections of material physically different from the main stock, for example, maps, music, manuscripts etc—seminar and laboratory collections, and collections bought, donated or bequested as separate entities. Some libraries appoint an officer to be especially responsible for the overall administration of special collections.

The first category of special collection, that in which the physical form of the material is different from that of the rest of the library stock, or in which the cataloguing and administration is different from that of the main stock, is dealt with by Francis J Brewer's 'Special problems of special collections' *College and research libraries* 23(3) May 1962. The conflict often met with in the treatment of such materials is that between the desire to keep the material together for ease of administration on the one hand, and, on the other hand, to arrange it alongside the subjects to which it refers (specially true of manuscript items, perhaps). Special equipment for storage and expertise for administration is, however, most effectively provided by dealing with these materials centrally.

Seminar collections are only to be distinguished from small departmental libraries by fine distinctions of definition. They may be described as workshop collections in laboratories, classrooms and staff rooms, with no full time librarian in charge of them. In some academic institutions, these collections are regarded as departmental equipment, and are paid for out of departmental funds. In others, the university library building itself is designed to house them, in small rooms adjacent to the main reading room so that they can be used by specific groups of students under the general supervision of the library staff. Indeed, seminars and tutorials can be carried out in these rooms quite conveniently. Wilson and Tauber deal with the administration and use of seminar collections in their book *The university library* (Columbia University Press, 1956).

CHAPTER SEVEN: RELATIONSHIP TO TEACHING AND RESEARCH

THE huge increases in enrolments in recent years, the urge to improve the quality of the teaching, and hence the quality of the output, the greater numbers of postgraduate research students and, of course, vastly increased teaching staff in universities and colleges—all of these things indicate corresponding pressures upon the library services. A pronounced feature of all university and much college teaching is the mode of teaching organization which combines independent 'self-organized' essay and project writing by the student with tutorials and small group seminars. This type of approach was well described by Lord Fulton's *Experiment in higher education* (Tavistock Institute, 1964). James F Govan believes that the developing situation makes it more than ever essential for librarians to regard their role as a dynamic one. Such, he says, is the increase in the amount of literature being produced, that the librarian must be the guide to, rather than the guardian of, knowledge; his article is entitled 'This is, indeed, the heart of the matter' *College and research libraries* 23(6) November 1962 467-472. To understand the huge problems posed by the increase in undergraduate numbers in universities, and the conflicting claims upon available finance that arise, one has only to read M Trow's 'The undergraduate dilemma in large state universities' *Universities quarterly* 21(1) December 1966 17-43.

If they are to understand the attitudes and objectives of research workers in their libraries, then librarians themselves must become more research oriented. The most obvious way of achieving this would be for librarians themselves to seek research experience. Given the present structures of academic and national libraries, it is rarely possible for library staff to obtain research experience 'on the job'; they must usually have obtained it prior to entry into the library profession. However, the increasing incidence of Office of Scientific and Technical Information awards to practising librarians for research into problems of library and information work, is now tending to increase the availability of 'on the job' research. More needs to be done, however. Librarians in active posts should have opportunities to develop their research interests, whether these are concerned with librarianship and information or with academic interests of their own. Librarians should, perhaps, be given the opportunity to secure secondment to teaching appointments for short periods, or obtain sabbatical leave for research purposes. The object of such measures would be to create in academic and national library staffs a greater sympathy with the aims and needs of the people they are serving. A M McAnally, in his article 'Social pressures and academic librarianship' ALA Bulletin 56(2) February 1962 159-164, claims that librarians are indeed, ignorant of the methods and the goals of education, and are lacking in the kind of intellectual stature in specialized fields which will encourage their users to have confidence in their abilities. W L Guttsman's 'Academic librarians and the structure of academic libraries' Libri 15(2) 1965 159-167 is well worth reading. Dr Guttsman, as a librarian, and previously as an academic and a researcher has himself academic credentials which make his thoughts on the problems of the librarian's approach to the needs of researchers almost uniquely authoritative.

THE STATUS OF LIBRARIANS WITHIN THEIR INSTITUTIONS
Writers on academic library themes in the American press often seem to be obsessed with questions of their status in the institution they are serving. It appears that many American academic librarians have not achieved anything like parity of esteem and salary with their colleagues in the teaching faculties. Their lack of intellectual stature is most frequently quoted as the root of their difficulty. D P Bergen, in his article 'Librarians and the bi-polarization of the academic enterprise' College and research libraries 24(6) November 1963 467-480, feels that there is a lack of rapport between teaching staff and library staff in the average American university, and that it is reaching serious proportions and having wholly undesirable effects upon the quality of the library service given. His conclusions, which place the bulk of the blame for the growth of such a situation upon the shoulders of the librarians, will not be popular with the latter, but there is no doubt much truth in his claim that librarians are so preoccupied

with the technical and administrative aspects of their work, that they are becoming incapable of making objective assessments of their role in the promotion of teaching and research. He sees the frequent conflict between library and faculty teaching staffs over the desirability or otherwise of creating departmental libraries as the most overt symptom of the growing difficulties, and he places much of the blame on the librarian who, he says, must be the party who concedes ground in such a situation if educational objectives are to be achieved. R E Moody supports him in his article 'Our academic library leadership: from the faculty?' *College and research libraries* 21(5) September 1960 362-368.

SUBJECT SPECIALIZATION BY LIBRARIANS
Bergen (*op cit*) and R S Smith 'The special library in the university' in *The two cultures* (Library Association, Reference Special and Information Section Annual Conference papers, 1961) note the need for more librarian/subject specialists with a deep knowledge of the way in which research proceeds. The subject specialist is not required to assist the library user only in fields directly relevant to his own specialisation. It would not be possible to provide enough specialists of this sort, even if it were desirable to do so. The point is that a person versed in the necessary research techniques in a specialist field is better able to make the necessary mental adjustments to the needs of researchers at the appropriate depth, than would be a person not so equipped.

Librarian/specialists can make a significant contribution to teaching at the department and faculty level, through the more intensive development of librarian/user relationships. Users come to have confidence in their librarians and, perhaps, more significant in terms of efficiency, weak library staff members are clearly shown up in their weakness, when they are expected to make a positive contribution to the work of specific departments, rather than provide a general service in a wholly centralized institution.

THE LIBRARY-COLLEGE CONCEPT
The newer concepts of 'self organized' teaching and learning, mentioned above, have focused attention upon the library as a central organ in the teaching process. With the strong development of audio-visual aids to teaching in the forms of teaching machines, film loops, slides, tapes, films, television recordings and

the associated hardware of closed circuit television, teaching, even in this self organized form, has become less dependent upon the printed word alone as the support and alternative to classroom teaching. The concept of the library-college is one recognition of the changes in the direction of educational methods. It is a concept of teaching being built not around the classroom or the laboratory, but around the library—though the library in this concept contains not only books and periodicals, but also the kinds of aids mentioned above, and as a consequence, is beginning to be called a 'learning resource centre'. The concept calls for students to be trained to work largely within the 'resource centre', drawing the teaching programmes, books and other audio-visual materials they need for their work, and using them in their own private study areas. Group tuition and tutorials are carried out in small rooms close to the library/resource centre. In his own study area, a student has the equipment to run through teaching programmes, and in the more advanced schemes has direct dialling access to a bank of stored videotapes of lectures and demonstrations, which he can have shown on his own personal viewer. While the student has access to whatever skilled help he needs, the basic fact is that, within the limits of a broad study programme laid down, he is on his own, with the library or 'learning resource centre' as his most accessible teacher.

Such a concept is obviously very exciting for a librarian to contemplate, since it is largely a vindication of all that librarians have been saying for a very long time about the importance of libraries as teaching instruments. However, it is still essentially an educationalist's concept, but one which does point to the need for librarians to keep themselves abreast of the latest in educational thinking, as well as professionally flexible enough to take the inevitable adjustments to the role of the library and of the librarian in their strides.

The library-college: contributions for American higher education at the Jamestown College Workshop 1965 (Philadelphia, Drexel Press, 1966) provides some of the basic reading about the concept. Norman W Beswick's 'Library-college: a new kind of library for an age when audio-visual aids may soon be as necessary as books' *Times educational supplement* March 3 1967 provides a useful summary of the most recent thinking.

LIBRARY USE STUDIES

One of the most basic matters which needs to be examined in deciding policy for a library is that which aims to find out what users need from their libraries, as distinct from what they actually are given. That librarians are keen to come to grips with these problems is clear from the large number of studies which have been made of library use, of sources from which students obtain their study materials, and of the attitudes of students to the library service to which they have access. R A Davis and C A Bailey have produced a *Bibliography of use studies* (Philadelphia, Graduate school of Library Science, Drexel Institute of Technology, 1964). The American Library Association's study of *Student use of libraries: an inquiry into the needs of students, libraries and the educational process: papers of a conference within a conference* July 16-18 1963 (American Library Association, 1964) focuses attention on the kinds of questions which need to be answered by use surveys. N N Nicholson and E Bartlett's 'Who uses university libraries?' *College and research libraries* 22(3) May 1962 217-222 provides a good example of what a questionnaire for this type of work should try to achieve. In planning to make use of the findings of surveys of users, it is important to realize that every institution has its own special problems—the physical location of the building, the modes of teaching, the personalities of the teaching staffs, the quality of the students, and the quality of the library and the library staff, will all tend to have largely unmeasurable effects upon the bias of particular surveys. Although bias need not make a survey any less useful for the situation in which it was planned, it does mean that reports of surveys in one college situation will have limited relevance to circumstances in another, however similar conditions in that other college might apparently be. Reports of surveys in other library situations, although interesting, do not provide a substitute for direct survey in a specific library, if information about its readers and their tastes is required.

Some general conclusions from recent surveys are possible, however, which do have a bearing on library policy in academic institutions. The most frequent criticisms of librarians seem to be that their hours of opening are not long enough, and, from undergraduates, that there is not sufficient duplication of the basic texts. On this last point, however, it is as well to recall that the Association of University Teachers survey *The university library* (AUT, 1964) asserts that students do not buy enough books themselves, but try instead to rely too much on the library for just the kinds of materials which they should be purchasing. In any survey of use, some questions on the book buying habits of students would be valuable.

NATIONAL LIBRARIES

The scope of the services offered to readers in national libraries varies considerably from library to library. In many countries, the national library is a 'last resort' collection, available only to those scholars who are able to provide proof that the materials they require to study are not available elsewhere. In some countries, however, the national library is also the library of a university (in Sweden, for example). However admirable an example of economy of effort this might seem, it is difficult to believe that in such circumstances the library is wholly successful in both roles. In some other countries, the national library is also a home reading collection on the public library model (in India and Singapore, for example). Similar criticisms must apply in this case.

Probably the point at which a national library enjoys the closest relationships with users is in the provision of a legislative reference service. J O Wilson's 'Legislative reference service' UNESCO *Bulletin for libraries* 18(4) July-August 1964 178-183 is a reprint of a paper first given at the UNESCO seminar on the development of national libraries in Asia and the Pacific area. Such a service should include not only the provision of factual data, but also research papers and assistance with speech writing, and the furnishing of bibliographical data.

TRAINING IN LIBRARY USE

Activities such as the kind of 'self-organized' work mentioned earlier, and the 'library-college' concept, require that academic students should have a high level of sophistication in the use of libraries and the associated bibliographical aids. It is regarded by many university and college librarians as one of their most important functions that they should provide training in the use of libraries.

The most basic method of providing orientation is the provision of a handbook describing the scope of the collections in the library, and information upon the methods of using the library and its associated services. Guided tours of the library are a feature of many national libraries and, indeed, are still the only form of assistance to readers practised in some universities. In many colleges and universities, the accent is now upon the provision of courses of instruction, not only to freshmen but also to postgraduate students, and even to staff members. An interesting development of this technique is the provision of a compulsory first year course for all students at the University of Stirling, known as ' approaches and methods ', which includes a section dealing with library services, and is examinable alongside other academic subjects at the end of the first year. Ellen Power has been looking into the ' state of the art ' of library instruction on behalf of the International Association of Technical University Libraries, and has written ' Instruction in the use of books and libraries ' *Libri* 14(3) 253-263. R E McCoy introduces the concept of instruction in the use of books and libraries using teaching machines in his article 'Automation in the freshman library' *Wilson library bulletin* 36(6) February 1962 468-470, 472, and H Pritchard speculates about ' Pre-arrival library instruction for college students' *College and research libraries* 26(4) July 1965 321-322.

REFERENCE LIBRARY SERVICE IN ACADEMIC LIBRARIES

One of the most frequent needs which is articulated in response to questionnaires on library use is for a more elaborate policy of reader assistance in academic libraries. In some academic libraries the old adage that the undergraduate must learn to find his own way round the library as an essential part of his education dies hard. The Association of University Teachers' survey *The university library* (AUT, 1964) underlines the need to develop an adequate level of reference service to all users, though it does point out that there are difficulties in deciding what constitutes such a service, since it is no part of the function of the library to do other people's research for them. Librarians in colleges of education and in public reference libraries will understand the point through their frequent contact with students who have been assigned ' projects ' by their tutors and who feel that there must inevitably be one convenient, concise source which the librarian can summarize for them in fulfilment of the project.

Another major difficulty in the provision of a reference service is that colleges and universities are not homogeneous in respect of the type of clientèle they serve. There are many levels of attainment to be catered for. Neal Harlow has developed this theme, and drawn attention to the problems, in two valuable articles 'Levels of need for library service in academic institutions' *College and research libraries* 24(5) September 1963 359-364, and 'An open skies system of academic library services' *Journal of education for librarianship* 2(4) 183-190.

The particular problem of service to the undergraduate student is one which many people feel is best dealt with by the provision of special collections for undergraduates (see page 77). Two articles in *College and research libraries* 26(3) May 1965 are by B S Page 'Library provision for undergraduates in England' (219-221), and S A McCarthy 'Library provision for undergraduates in the United States' (222-224).

CHAPTER EIGHT : CO-OPERATION

PERHAPS one of the most important aspects of the development of schemes of co-operation has been those measures designed to improve the standards of the collections of foreign literature within a country. National libraries can no longer claim to be fully comprehensive, if indeed they were ever so able; even the largest of them are obliged to concede that they are unable to collect everything they would like to have. The existence of the National Library of Medicine and the National Library of Agriculture, and of the *National union catalog*, in the United States, is visible indication that the Library of Congress, for all its vast resources, is itself limited.

Schemes of co-operative acquisition have, therefore, been developed in some countries to attempt to produce at least some semblance of comprehensiveness in foreign literature. Three most important schemes are, The Farmington Plan, The Scandia Plan, and the scheme operated by the Deutsche Forschungsgemeinschaft. Other efforts to take the load off a national library involve the development of schemes of co-operative acquisition, on a subject specialist basis, of the publications of the home country as well. Taken together, such schemes as these significantly improve the stocks of research literature in a country. In the Netherlands the organization of a national co-operative acquisition system for Dutch publications has been designed with the intention of relieving the Royal and National Library of the obligation to collect Dutch publications comprehensively, in order that it may be free to concentrate upon the purchase of foreign literature.

To make schemes such as these successful, it follows that there must exist a high degree of goodwill and mutual trust among the libraries joining in the co-operative activity. This goodwill needs to extend to the international plane, as well as the national, as the co-operative machinery grows in complexity. Meetings such as the 1958 Symposium on National Libraries in Europe held in Vienna (the papers of which form the volume *National libraries:*

their problems and prospects (UNESCO, 1960), and the Regional Seminar on the Development of National Libraries in Asia and the Pacific Area (the papers of which were summarized in UNESCO *Bulletin for libraries* 18(4) July-August 1964) are important as a means of creating the atmosphere of interdependence so necessary for successful co-operation.

The International Federation of Library Association's section, International Association of Technical University Libraries, which was established in 1955, and the same Federation's National and Universities Section, do a great deal of work in fostering the spirit of international co-operation. Nationally, such bodies as SCONUL (The Standing Conference of National and University Libraries), and the Association of Research Libraries in the United States, the University and Research Library section of the Library Association, and the Association of College and Research Libraries, which is a section of the American Library Association, do similar work.

SCONUL

Detailed reviews of the activities of this organization appear in *Libri*, for example in 7(1) 1956 41-44 and 12(1) 1962 56-60. K W Humphreys, who provides these reviews has also contributed to *Library world* 67(782) August 1965 on the same subject.

SCONUL was founded in 1950 ' to promote the work of national and university libraries '. This it attempts to do in various ways. It holds regular meetings of the representatives of the national libraries (widely defined to include The Public Record Office and John Rylands Library, as well as The British Museum and the Science Library), the librarians of the British universities, and of several major colleges within and without the university structure. A recent development of major significance has been the growth of staff training and short courses.

There are a number of special committees, in addition to the executive committee, and one of them, the Co-operation in Acquisitions Committee, is of particular relevance in the field of library co-operation. This committee has examined the possibility of operating a ' Farmington Plan ' (see below) in the United Kingdom, and has surveyed the coverage of a number of specific types of foreign material in British libraries, for example, history, classics and medical periodicals, Russian periodicals in cover to cover translation, and American literature (*see* B R Crick 'A survey of literature resources in the United Kingdom for the teaching of American history in the universities' *Journal of documentation* 14(2) June 1958 109).

THE ASSOCIATION OF RESEARCH LIBRARIES
This organization, representing the views of the large American libraries, came into being in 1931 with the object of developing and increasing the usefulness of research collections in the United States.

THE SCANDINAVIAN ASSOCIATION OF RESEARCH LIBRARIES
This organization, which has a similar scope to the Association of Research Libraries, includes, however, both individual and corporate members from all of the countries in Scandinavia.

CO-OPERATIVE ACQUISITION
A number of major schemes exist in various parts of the world, designed to ensure that particular countries or groups of countries achieve something like total coverage of general or specific fields of literature. Although there are many common features about their modes of working, it is worthwhile describing each in some detail and providing further references since they are favourite subjects for examination questions.

The Background Material Scheme: Developed by the Joint Standing Committee on Library Co-operation of the Association of University Teachers, the scheme has the aim of dividing up the field of acquisition of early printed books into units of ten years. That is to say, various participating libraries agree to make themselves responsible for the purchase of material published before 1800, on the basis of each covering a period of ten years. An individual library thus agrees to purchase all those books which come on to the market which were originally published between two specified dates, for example a period such as 1761-1770. The organizational arrangements of the scheme are described in an article in *British universities annual 1964* (Association of University Teachers, 1964), and a statement from the administering committee appeared in the *Library Association record* 69(10) October 1967 356.

The Farmington Plan: Established in 1948, and named after

the town in Connecticut where preliminary discussions leading to the formulation of the plan were held. The scheme is administered by the Association of Research Libraries, with the aim of improving the supply of library material published outside the United States into the country. To further this end, certain large research libraries in the United States have agreed to make themselves responsible for the collection of all significant book and pamphlet material appearing either in specific subjects within specific countries, or else for all material, irrespective of subject, from a particular country or country group, depending upon the size and nature of the book trade in different areas of the world. The country basis is usually adopted for those countries whose language problems are such that few American libraries are prepared to handle them, or, as already stated, for those countries in which the book trade is poorly organized. In most cases, assignment of subjects is carried out on the basis of associating such work with libraries which already have a strong coverage of the subject in question.

The acquisition of materials under the terms of the plan is effected by the appointment of agents—usually leading booksellers —who are advised by librarians, appointed by the plan, to forward to the participating libraries the most significant items published in the country of origin. The agencies were originally established by the Association of Research Libraries, but it is now possible for individual libraries to appoint their own agents and advisers if they so wish.

The *Vosper-Talmadge report* of 1959 was a most significant event, which resulted in the creation of a much expanded plan. Previous to 1959, only Western Europe was covered to anything like an acceptable degree. Material acquired is reported to the *National union catalog* by participating libraries, and made available through inter-library loan schemes on a national basis. Basic readings are the *Farmington Plan handbook 1953*, which was not entirely superseded by the second edition which appeared in 1961, and which also contains a summary of the *Vosper-Talmadge report*. Dr Vosper's article ' Farmington redivivus ' ASLIB *Proceedings* 11(11) November 1959 327-334 is also useful.

SCANDIA Plan: The plan is basically similar to Farmington, and had its genesis in a scheme developed originally by the four largest research libraries in Sweden in the year 1955, to co-operate in the acquisition of foreign material. In 1956, the first steps were taken to extend the scheme to the other Scandinavian countries. The plan is based upon the known subject and linguistic interests of libraries. The plan began by covering the humanities, and later extended into other subject fields. An important by-product of the plan has been the improvement of relations between libraries of similar interest in the various Scandinavian countries—the parliamentary libraries in the several countries have begun their own sub-plan for the improved collection and dissemination of parliamentary papers.

Deutsche Forschungsgemeinschaft (Co-operative Procurement Scheme): Besides acting as a central clearing house for national and international exchanges, and for inter-library co-operation, the organization has taken steps to improve the availability of foreign scientific literature throughout Western Germany.

A plan has been devised whereby the larger German libraries have been assigned a ' special collection field ', and provided with funds from the central agency to enable them to purchase the most important foreign scientific books in their field which have been published since 1939 (or, in some areas, since 1930). Periodicals are also covered by the scheme on the same terms. The participating libraries are, of course, also expected to acquire German material published in their own field very intensively. The books acquired under the terms of the scheme are selected by the libraries concerned, but the periodicals are purchased as a result of a central direction. Inter-library co-operative machinery is associated with this plan, and support is provided for the creation of union catalogues on a regional basis, and of union lists of periodicals and indexes to periodical literature.

A pamphlet *German Research Association: structure and functions* is available freely from the Deutsche Forschungsgemeinschaft. L S Thompson has described the operations of the scheme in his ' Subject specialisation in German research libraries ' in *Farmington Plan survey . . .final report* (Association of Research Libraries, 1959)—the official title of the *Vosper-Talmadge report*. Another reference of great value is H H Hoffman ' Cooperative acquisitions in German research libraries ' *Library quarterly* 34(3) July 1964 249-251.

CO-OPERATIVE STORAGE AND STORAGE LIBRARIES

This can take the form of a number of libraries combining to purchase cheap, accessible storage areas for the storage of their little used material, with facilities for its swift return in time of need. Such stores, where they exist, work in one of two principal ways. Either the co-operating libraries combine to rent space, which they then use as extensions of their own stores, or else they set up an organization to administer the store as a cohesive unit, vesting the title in any materials stored jointly in the names of all the co-operating libraries. In some systems, the store set up in this latter way also has its own funds, to enable the staff operating it to buy additional background material to round off existing holdings, or extend the range of the material stored.

There is another method of co-operative storage which does not call for the purchase or rent of additional space. This method is to arrange exchanges of material between participating libraries on some pre-determined basis, usually by subject, with the receiving library either adding the material received to their own stored material, or else returning it to the sender in cases of duplicated material already in the store. Such material can then be disposed of with the security of knowing that, in the event of the library needing it in the future, one of the co-operating libraries will be able to supply it from their stock. The storage scheme operated by the law libraries associated with the University of London runs along similar lines to that outlined above.

Whichever method is adopted in co-operative storage, the purpose is the same—to alleviate pressure on storage accommodation in individual libraries, without running the risk of reducing the standards of service, and at the same time cutting to a minimum the high cost of storing library materials.

The Center for Research Libraries (formerly the Mid-West Inter-Library Center) is, perhaps, the best known and best documented of these storage library concepts. The center, while allowing for those libraries which wish to retain title in stored material by offering space on a rental basis, is principally interested in the collation of material sent to it. Material surplus to requirements can then be disposed of with the consent of the donating library. Such a scheme ensures the maximum of economy in storage charges. The basic reference on the center is *The report of a survey with an outline of programs and policies* (Chicago, The Center for Research Libraries, 1965).

Other references to the subject of storage libraries include H J Harrar 'Co-operative storage warehouses' *College and research libraries* 25(1) January 1964 37-43, and Jerrold Orne's 'Storage and deposit libraries' *College and research libraries* 21(6) November 1960 446-452. The Harrar article describes in detail the operations of the major American storage libraries; the second article, by Orne, discusses the philosophy behind their establishment, and also questions the values in book selection and utilization which caused them to be established.

THE NATIONAL LENDING LIBRARY FOR SCIENCE AND TECHNOLOGY

Though not, in fact, a co-operative storehouse, the NLL does have some features in common with such institutions. It will accept files of little used periodicals for permanent storage if it does not already have them available in its own stock. It does, thereby, not only ensure the preservation of rare material, but also sees that full use is made of it through its availability to a wider circle of libraries and library users than is possible in libraries not so fully geared to the national inter-library lending system.

Another reflection of the co-operative store philosophy in the NLL is that, by its collection on a world-wide basis of periodicals in a wide range of subjects, both within and, more recently, without the science and technology field, individual libraries are able to concentrate upon primary needs, rather than building up expensive files of secondary material. Such libraries are still secure in the knowledge that the secondary material and material in foreign languages can be obtained quickly when required from the National Lending Library.

THE NATIONAL LIBRARY IN THE CO-OPERATIVE NETWORK

In many countries, the national library is at the centre of all bibliographic activity and library endeavour in the country. In the more advanced countries, where the build-up of library resources has taken place over a longer period, this concept does not always hold good, because there are many libraries which share the leadership function between them. As indicated in chapter one, however, the planning of national library systems in the developing countries has often given priority to the national library itself as the cornerstone of the whole system. C D Wormann has examined the role of the national library in relation to co-operation in his article ' Co-operation of national libraries with other libraries in the same and other countries ' UNESCO *Bulletin for libraries* 18(4) July-August 1964 165-171. The way in which the British Museum sees the development of its role in inter-library co-operation was outlined by F C Francis in ' The contribution of the national library to the modern outlook in library services ' ASLIB *Proceedings* 10(11) November 1958 267-275.

Some national libraries act as the national clearinghouses for inter-library loans (this role was specifically abrogated by the British Museum in 1927, after a Kenyon Committee recommendation that it should take it on). Exchange of publications is also an activity which many national libraries take responsibility for. UNESCO has been active in promoting the flow of publication exchange on an international basis, and has also assisted in the establishment of micro-recording projects which have made available to libraries material which was previously inaccessible. National libraries have played a very large part in making the originial materials available for micro-recording.

ACADEMIC LIBRARIES

The *Parry report* is the most comprehensive survey of the co-operative activity of academic libraries to be published in recent years. Several sections of the report deal exclusively with the problems and patterns of co-operation in these libraries.

Besides some informal schemes of co-operation based upon known subject specializations, the production of union lists of periodicals, and the ' background scheme ' described earlier, the pattern of integration of the academic libraries into the national scheme of co-operation does not require any special treatment here, since they have always played a full part in the formal machinery of co-operation in the United Kingdom. The most recent source of reference, providing an appreciation of the position of the academic library in the formal co-operative machinery of the country, is G Jefferson *Library co-operation* (Deutsch, 1968).

Technical college libraries have often been prime movers in local schemes of technical information provision and co-operation. Schemes such as NANTIS (Nottingham and Nottinghamshire Technical Information Service), and TALIC (Tyneside Association of Libraries for Industry and Commerce), usually have strong representation of technical college library interests. A number of colleges are bases for the industrial liaison officers attached to the Ministry of Technology. These centres provide a link between industry, colleges and the various government research establishments, and enable people and organizations with technical information problems to be helped in the most practical way. Technical college libraries which are associated with colleges having such centres are often heavily used by the officers of the centre and their clients. In this way the value of good library services can be demonstrated at a time when it will do the most good—when someone has information problems which the library helps to solve. A number of municipal and county public libraries have taken their desire to ensure that there will be adequate co-operation between their libraries and those of technical colleges within their area of service to a conclusion, which seems to be the logical one, of complete integration of the public library technical service with that of the nearby technical colleges. Such a practice operates in Hertfordshire county, Belfast city and in Nottinghamshire county, for example.

Colleges of education libraries derive considerable benefits from the institute of education library of the university with which they are associated, and also from local public libraries. The introduction of more broadly based 'academic' programmes in the process of educating students for the teaching profession calls for the development of even closer links with other local libraries, at least until the college of education library is able to provide for the bulk of its own needs in such fields.

INDEX

Acquisitions 64
American university libraries 27
Association of College and Research Libraries 90
Association of Research Libraries 90, 91, 92
Association of Teachers in Technical Institutes 34
Association of University Teachers 22, 43, 61, 70, 86, 91
Audio-visual materials 83
Australian university libraries 51
Automation 16, 39, 48, 53, 87

Background material scheme 91
Ballinger, Sir, John 18
Bandinet, Bulkeley 25
Bibliotheca Celtica 7, 18
Bibliothèque Nationale 8, 11, 17
Bodley, Sir Thomas 12, 19, 25
Book selection 64
Boston Public Library 15
Bradshaw, Henry 24
British Museum, 91
rules 12
British Museum Library 8, 11,12, 36, 39, 40, 57, 63, 90
British Museum Act 1963 13, 14, 36
British national bibliography 49

Cambridge University Library 19, 24
Cataloguing 12, 39, 49, 80
Center for Research Libraries 94
Classification 15, 40, 49
Closed circuit television 84
Colleges of education libraries 34, 87, 97
Columbia University 51
Conference of the Universities of the UK 52
Co-operation 8, 9, 16, 89
Co-operative acquisition 91
Co-operative storage 94
Copyright Act 1709 19
Council for National Academic Awards 31, 60
Council on Library Resources 39

Dainton, Dr F S 14
Department of Education and Science 14
Departmental libraries 83
Deutsche Forschungsgemeinschaft 89, 93
Dewey decimal classification 49
Divisional libraries 75
Donations 69
Duke Humfrey's Library 25
Duplication, Textbooks 85

Equipment 51
Evans, Dr Luther 16
Exchanges 63, 65, 96

Faculty of Advocates 17
Farmington Plan 16, 66, 89, 90, 92
Finance 36, 38, 44
Fittings 51
Foreign literature 89
Francis, Sir Frank 37
Franklyn, Benjamin 14
French university libraries 28
Friends of the National Libraries 39, 46
Functions, National libraries 7, 8
University libraries 21

German university libraries 28
Government, National libraries 36
University libraries 41

Harvard University Library 51, 76
Hours of opening 47
Hungarian National Library 7
Hyde, Thomas 25

Illinois University Library 51
Industrial liaison officers 97
Insurance 46
International Association of Technical University Libraries 87
International Federation of Library Associations 20, 90
Italy, University libraries 22

James, Thomas 25
Jefferson, President Thomas 15

Jenkinson, Francis 24
John Rylands Library 90

Kenyon report 96

Learning resource centres 84
Legal deposit 2, 19, 20, 66
Lenin Library 11, 20, 38
Library architecture 52
Library Association 11, 25, 34, 90
Library-college 23, 83, 84, 86
Library Company of Philadelphia 14
Library of Congress 8, 11, 14, 16, 20, 37, 38, 41, 63, 89
Library of Congress Classification 49
Library Technology Project 46
Loans policy 47
London University Library 26, 94

McLeish, Archibald 16
Madan, Falconer 25
Management 59
Manuscripts 8
Ministry of Technology 97
Modular planning 52
Mumford, L Quincy 16
Myres, J N L 25

National Central Library 14
National libraries 7, 86
National Diet Library, Japan 7
National Lending Library for Science and Technology 14, 57, 95
National Library of Agriculture 89
National Library of Australia 21
National Library of Belgium 11
National Library of Canada 21
National Library of Hungary 7
National Library of Medicine 89
National Library of New Zealand 14, 21
National Library of Nigeria 21
National Library of Scotland 7, 17, 37, 38, 40
National Library of Scotland Act 17
National Library of Wales 7, 8, 18, 19, 36
National Reference Library for Science and Invention 14, 36
National Science Foundation 16
National union catalog 16, 40, 89
National Union of Students 47
Newbery Library, Chicago 9
New York Public Library 68

Nicholson, W B 25
Nottingham University Library 74

Office of Scientific and Technical Information 81
Open University 26, 29
Ordinance de Montpellier 19
Oxford University Library 19, 24

Panizzi, Antonio 12, 36
Parry report 22, 23, 30, 42, 43, 45, 65, 79, 96
Parry, Thomas *see Parry report*
Personnel management 59
Planning 51
Polytechnics 31, 32, 70
Princeton University 78
Programmed learning 84
Public libraries 87
Public Record Office 90
Putnam, Herbert 15, 36

Report of the Committee on Libraries see Parry report
Research 66, 67, 81
Rider, Fremont 51
Robbins report 30, 31, 34

Salaries 62
Savage, Ernest 25
Scandia Plan 89, 92
Scandinavian Association of Research Libraries 91
Science Museum Library 14, 90
Scottish university libraries 26
Seminar collections 80, 81
Sheffield Postgraduate School of Librarianship 49
Site selection 54
Sloane, Sir Hans 12
South African university libraries 29
Special collections 72
Spofford, Ainsworth 15
Staff 59
Standards 33, 80
Standing Conference of National and University Libraries 61, 90
Star Chamber 19
Stationers Company 19
Stirling University 87
Stock 64
Storage libraries 94
Surveys of library use 85
Swedish university libraries 28

99

Student use of libraries 85
Subject specialization 61

Teaching machines 87
Technical college libraries 30
Technical services 39
Textbooks 78, 85
Training in library use 86
Trinity College, Dublin 19, 24
Tutorials 67, 84

Undergraduate libraries 77, 88
UNESCO Symposium on National Libraries in Europe 9
Universal decimal classification 49
University Grants Committee 21, 33, 41

University libraries *see* under names of individual countries *eg* German university libraries
University library functions 53
University Microfilms 77
University of California (San Diego) Library 53
Use studies 85

Vosper-Talmadge report 92

Washington University Library 79
Watterson, George 15
Williams, Sir John 18

Yale University Library 51